Navajo Code Talkers

Navajo
Code
Talkers

Nathan Aaseng

WALKER & COMPANY
NEW YORK

First published in the United States of America in 1992
by Walker Publishing Company, Inc.; first paperback
edition published in 2000.

Published simultaneously in Canada by Fitzhenry and Whiteside,
Markham, Ontario L3R 4T8

Library of Congress Cataloging-in-Publication Data
Aaseng, Nathan.
Navajo code talkers / Nathan Aaseng.
p.   cm.
Includes bibliographical references and index.
Summary: Describes how the American military in World War II used
a group of Navajo Indians to create an indecipherable code based on
their native language.
ISBN 0-8027-8182-9 (C).—ISBN 0-8027-8183-7 (R)
1. World War, 1939–1945—Cryptography—Juvenile literature.
2. World War, 1939–1945—Participation, Indian—Juvenile
literature.   3. Navajo Indians—Juvenile literature.   [1. World War,
1939–1945—Participation, Indian.   2. Cryptography.   3. Navajo
Indians.   4. Indians of North America.]   I. Title.
D810.C88A24   1992
940.54′8673—dc20   92-11408
CIP
AC
ISBN 0-8027-7589-6 (paperback)

Book design by Shelli Rosen

Printed in the United States of America

2   4   6   8   10   9   7   5   3   1

Contents

CHINA

Chung King

INDIA

BURMA

Hanoi

Hong Kong

Manila

FRENCH
INDO
CHINA

Saigon

BRITISH
MALAYA

DUTCH

SUMATRA

Singapore

EAST

INDIAN OCEAN

JAVA

INDIES

SEA OF JAPAN

Hiroshima

Nagasaki

JAPAN

Tokyo

Okinawa

Iwo Jima

MARIANA
ISLANDS

Saipan

GUAM

PHILIPPINE
SEA

PHILIPPINES

BORNEO

CELEBES

Buna

NEW
GUINEA

Port Moresby

AUSTRALIA

ALEUTIAN ISLANDS

PACIFIC OCEAN

MIDWAY

HAWAIIAN ISLANDS

Pearl Harbor

WAKE

CAROLINE
ISLANDS

MARSHALL
ISLANDS

GILBERT
ISLANDS

Tarawa

Rabaul

SOLOMON
ISLANDS

Guadalcanal

Navajo Code Talkers

▶ 1 ◀

War of Words

U.S. MARINES ADVANCING ACROSS the Pacific island of Saipan during World War II hacked their way through lush, tangled wilderness and dense sugar-cane plantations. Steep ravines and rugged volcanic mountains barred their path.

There was no such thing as a battle line for these soldiers. Danger lay not just ahead of them, but also to the side and possibly even behind. The unseen guns of the enemy were hidden by the pitch dark of night, by the thick tropical vegetation, or by the walls of caves that burrowed deep into the mountains.

Each soldier knew his next step might be his last. The rustling of leaves a few yards away in any direction was as likely to be an enemy as a friend.

On the extreme left flank of the American forces trying to capture Saipan, a battalion of marines ran into blistering volleys of fire from determined Japanese defenders. In the furious struggle that followed, neither side gained any ground. One morning, however, the marines noticed a strange silence along the enemy front. Cautiously scouting the terrain, they discovered that the Japanese had abandoned the area and retreated to new defensive positions. The marines crept forward.

Suddenly, artillery shells exploded all around them. Hugging the ground to protect themselves from flying shrapnel, the marines soon discovered that the bombardment was coming from far behind them, obviously from their own artillery units!

Those American gunners were following orders to blast away at the Japanese in those positions. They had no way of knowing that the Japanese had pulled out and that U.S. Marines now occupied the area. Quickly, one of the marines radioed to headquarters, frantically calling for a stop to the bombardment.

Now the artillery commanders faced a knotty problem. The Japanese were in general far more fluent in English than the Americans were in Japanese. They often pretended to be Americans and sent out false radio messages in English. If the receiver believed these message, traps could be baited and entire battle plans disrupted. Was this one of those fake messages, sent out to halt a much needed artillery attack? Unfortunately, in the confusion of the scattered battle lines, there was no quick way of finding out just what was true.

The report sounded suspicious and was ignored. American artillery continued to lob explosives at the marines. Another urgent radio message crackled over the wire, pleading with the artillery to stop firing on the marines.

This time headquarters sent a message back: "Do you have a Navajo there?"

There was, in fact, a member of a specially trained group of Navajo Indians in the battalion. The Navajo rushed to the radio. Speaking in a special code developed from his native language, this Navajo sent the message to another Navajo manning the radio at headquarters. The decoded message given to officers at headquarters was identical to the original message that had come from the artillery target area, and this time there could be no mistake. The code was unbreakable; no one but a Navajo member of the U.S. Marine Corps could have made that call. The bombardment stopped immediately.

The plight of the marine battalion on Saipan was just one of countless incidents in which the Navajo code talkers, as they were called, saved the day in World War II. More than 400 code talkers fanned out among marine units in the Pacific, using their language to fight the enemy. Because of them, the marines held a critical advantage over the Japanese. Their frontline soldiers could exchange communications with their top commanders quickly, without fear of their messages being intercepted. The Japanese could not.

In answering the call of duty in World War II, the Navajos provided a vivid example of amazing grace. They set aside bitterness and risked their lives to defend the very government that had brutally enslaved their grandparents. These twentieth-century Navajos fought for the United States, the country whose original attitude toward Native Americans was expressed by one of the Navajos' conquer-

Navajo members of the U.S. Marines Corps send out a message in a special unbreakable code from a South Pacific jungle.

ors, General William T. Sherman: "The more we kill this year, the less we will have to kill next year. Their attempts at civilization are simply ridiculous."[1]

The Navajos descended from a loosely connected group of people, known as Athapascans, who dwelt in Alaska and northern Canada. Thousands of years ago, the Navajos broke away from their northern kin. They moved south and eventually settled in the arid lands that are now Arizona, New Mexico, and southern Utah.

The Navajos supported a fairly stable population of about 10,000 people, primarily through agriculture, until the arrival of Spanish adventurers in the eighteenth century. Spanish explorations opened the way for settlers from Mexico to move into the region. Navajo relations with their new neighbors degenerated quickly. Mexicans kidnapped Navajo children to work as servants. The Navajo countered with raids against the Mexicans.

In the mid–nineteenth century, the arrival of fortune-seekers from the eastern United States, many of whom passed through on their way to the California gold rush, brought an even more devastating clash of cultures. Neither group understood or trusted the other. U.S. officials made the mistake of assuming that the Navajo people had leaders who governed the entire tribe. When they talked one or two Navajos into signing treaties, they expected all Navajos to abide by them. In fact, the Navajos consisted of many widely scattered clans, each operating independently. Most of them had not signed these treaties and saw no reason to be bound by them. Those Navajos who did sign were angered at how frequently the treaty promises were blatantly ignored.

Problems between Navajos and the United States escalated into violence in the early 1860s. The U.S. Army decided to crush the Navajos' spirit once and for all. General James Carleton ordered Colonel Kit Carson into Navajo land with brutal instructions: Force the Navajo into the stark choice of surrender or starvation. In 1863, Carson's troops trampled and burned Navajo cornfields and vegetable gardens. They chopped down the orchards, killed the wild game, burned the firewood, and drove off or slaughtered the sheep. They burned Navajo villages to the ground and killed any Navajos who resisted.

Homeless, without food for the winter, most Navajos had no choice but to surrender. They were rounded up and driven like cattle on a 300-mile trek to Fort Sumner in eastern New Mexico. The Long Walk, as the Navajos call it, lasted three weeks. The Navajos had no idea where they were going or why they were going there. They were cold and hungry. Old people and tiny infants died along the way.

The plan was for the Navajos to be "reformed" at Fort Sumner. In reality, the fort was little more than a concentration camp. As many as 2,000 Navajos died of hunger and illness during their four-year exile.

While many Navajos were shattered by the experience, others refused to give up hope. They reminded themselves how their ancestors had survived bleak times, and they steeled themselves against hardship. Since all Navajos were lumped together in Fort Sumner and endured the

Legendary trailblazer Kit Carson carried out the U.S. Army's plan to evict the Navajos from their lands. (COURTESY OF THE LIBRARY OF CONGRESS)

hardship together, they began to think of themselves, for the first time, as one people—the Navajo nation.

In 1868, the Navajos were allowed to return to their homes on the condition that they never again fight against the United States or Mexico or against other Native Americans. Most of the Navajo clans lived in remote areas, on land that was too dry for intensive farming. That proved to be most fortunate for them. American settlers were not particularly interested in this land, and so the Navajos were one of the few Native American groups granted their homelands as their reservation.

The misery and injustice of that period of imprisonment have been etched in the memory of the Navajos. The Long Walk made such an impact on them that they reckon all dates from that event. Small children are taught the story of the Long Walk. A century after it, one author found that older Navajos could hardly speak for a few minutes without mentioning that terrible event.

Yet the sons and grandsons of those who endured the Long Walk at the hands of the U.S. government came to the defense of that government in 1917: Many Navajos enlisted in the army and fought for the United States in World War I. But their contributions were ignored. Although the federal government granted citizenship to Native Americans in 1924, the state laws of Arizona and New Mexico continued to deny Navajos the right to vote.

In the late 1930s, world peace was again threatened. After listening to radio reports of the aggressive military ventures of Japan and Germany, the Navajos did not hesitate to take action. Undaunted by the United States' past treatment of their people, the Navajo leadership issued the following statement on June 6, 1940, a year and a half before the United States entered World War II: "We resolve that the Navajo Indians stand ready as they did in 1918, to aid and defend our Government and Constitution against all subversive and armed conflict."[2]

When war did break out, Navajo men headed for the reservation agency to report for duty. Unfamiliar with the U.S. military, many of them brought their own rifles. Out of a total population of approximately 55,000, more than 3,600 Navajos overcame the bitter memory of the Long Walk and joined the U.S. armed forces in World War II. Many others attempted to join but were not accepted because of health problems or language barriers.

More than 300 Navajo men gave their lives for their country in that war. General Sherman would have been shocked to look into the future and see the Navajo Indians in the forefront of America's fight for freedom in World War II.

Of all the contributions made by the Navajos in this war effort, none was more valuable than the work of the select group of men who became known as the Navajo code talkers. The code talkers' impact on the war was one final irony, one last undeserved blessing that the United States received from these mistreated people. Many of the government-supported schools for the Navajos had strictly insisted that the students *not* speak the Navajo language.

Navajo culture was to be ignored; all instruction was to be in English.

U.S. servicemen were fortunate that the attempt to replace the Navajo language with English did not succeed. Many of them owe their lives to those Navajos who used their language to fight for the United States.

► 2 ◄

Needed: An Unbreakable Code

RAPID, SECRET COMMUNICATION IS as important to any military operation as weapons and ammunition. Those who plan strategy need up-to-the-minute reports from the front lines in order to understand what needs to be done. Those in the front lines needed a constant flow of instructions so that their actions are coordinated with those of the rest of the army. If any of this communication falls into enemy hands, however, the enemy can make plans to counter whatever is coming.

Sending messages between armies or between sections of armies has always been a risky business because of the danger that the enemy might intercept the messages. More than 2,000 years ago, military leaders began devising ways to disguise important messages. In the fifth century B.C., a Greek exile in Persia learned of the Persians' plans to invade the Greek states. He wrote out a message of warning on a wooden tablet and then covered the surface of the tablet with wax before sending it by messenger to Sparta.

To all appearances the tablet was blank, and the messenger was allowed to proceed to Sparta. After a great deal of puzzlement, the Spartans discovered the secret of the tablet. Warned of the invasion, they sent out troops to stop the Persian advance. The secret message helped save Greek civilization from certain defeat.

Over the centuries, a great number of clever codes have been developed by military people to disguise their messages. Codes use symbols to represent the messages' true meaning. They make sense only to someone who knows the code and so reveal nothing to an enemy even if they are intercepted. One of the most common code forms has been the cryptogram. In a cryptogram, each letter stands for a different letter. For example, whenever a "P" appears, it really means "E."

For many centuries, cryptograms were difficult to decipher, or break. Without knowing the code, people did not know which cryptogram letter matched up with which real letter. In the nineteenth century, however, a German officer named Kasiski developed a table known as a frequency chart. This told how often, on the average, a certain letter appeared in a given number of words. In the English language, for example, the letter "E" is the most commonly used letter, occurring an average of 591 times per 1,000 words. In those same 1,000 words, the letter "C" appears an average of 124 times. The letter "Z" occurs only 3 times, and so on. Knowledge of the frequency with which letters occur in a language made it much easier to guess what each letter in a cryptogram stood for. After Kasiski, codes were suddenly much easier to break.

Once frequency charts became common knowledge, devising and breaking codes became something of an art form. Every major military organization assigned some of its members to try and develop unbreakable codes and others to break new enemy codes. It was understood that any advantage that could be gained in communicating secret messages could make the difference between winning and losing a war.

From its shocking opening volley, the war in the Pacific of 1941–45 depended heavily on the quality of secret communications. Unlike most large-scale wars, which have been fought on landmasses, the Allied forces (composed primarily of U.S. troops, along with British, Australian, Filipino, and other troops) battled the Japanese on hundreds of islands spread out over thousands of miles of Pacific Ocean. Speedy, reliable communication between such isolated outposts was difficult even in peacetime. Deploying troops and supplies over this sprawling theater of war without tipping off the enemy was a special challenge. The side that could send secret messages more quickly and effectively would hold an enormous advantage.

Japan held this advantage in the first days of the war and made devastating use of it. In late 1941, when Japan and the United States were still at peace, Japan organized a powerful strike force in the middle of the Pacific Ocean. Six large aircraft carriers turned off their radios and closed in on the United States' main Pacific Ocean naval base at Pearl Harbor, Hawaii. Despite ominous threats from Japan's military, the military command at Pearl Harbor was unaware that the base was the main target. On December 7,

The half-submerged U.S.S. ARIZONA lies in ruins in Pearl Harbor after Japan's surprise attack on December 7, 1941. (COURTESY OF NATIONAL ARCHIVES)

1941, Japanese warplanes roared out of the early morning skies over Hawaii, catching the Americans totally off guard. Only a handful of U.S. aircraft got off the ground to challenge the attack. More than 3,000 U.S. soldiers were killed. Five warships sank; hundreds of planes were destroyed. American military strength in the Pacific was crippled.

Japan's armies then stormed through much of the Pacific, targeting rich storehouses of raw materials for their industries: the Philippine Islands, Hong Kong, Malaysia, the Dutch East Indies, New Guinea. Looking ahead to the inevitable counterattack from the United States, they attacked strategic military bases in island chains such as the Marshalls, the Marianas, the Gilberts, and the Solomons.

The United States had few weapons with which to combat this onslaught, especially after the Pearl Harbor disaster. The forces left in the Pacific could not possibly fortify every position that might come under attack. All they could do was play a guessing game—try to mass their strength in just the right place at just the right time to repel the next enemy attack.

The best way to find out what the Japanese were up to was to read their mail and listen to their phone calls. American intelligence units showed an astounding ability to intercept messages and break codes. Just as the war was beginning, the United States had broken Japan's top secret Purple Code, which the Japanese had thought uncrackable. Throughout the rest of the war, secrets stolen from Japanese messages gave the United States a good idea of what to prepare for.

The Japanese, however, enjoyed the same advantage. Their military intelligence was so skilled at tapping American communications and breaking codes that the United States could keep few secrets. No matter how often the Americans changed codes, their messages were easily decoded. According to one war analyst, "Military communications were made available to the enemy like sand sifting through a sieve."[3] So Japan often had advance warning of where U.S. troops were, where they were going, and when they would get there.

With neither side able to keep a secret in the combat zone, battles were decided by the sheer strength of the forces in the field. In the early days of the war, Japan enjoyed overwhelming military superiority. Its armies swept to victory after stunning victory, including the capture of more than 12,000 American soldiers on the Bataan Peninsula in the Philippines. By the spring of 1942, Japan ruled most of the Pacific Ocean, all the way down to the doorstep of Australia.

While probing for a strategy to use against Japan, U.S. military leaders pondered how they could turn the communications battle in their favor. Japan continued to break every code the Americans tried. Somehow, the United States had to find a way to send messages to and from the troops rapidly, without announcing the plans to the enemy.

While some of the best military minds in the country were wrestling with the problem of devising an unbreakable code, a civilian came up with the answer. Philip Johnston, a civil engineer for the city of Los Angeles, happened across a news story about an armored division stationed in Louisiana that was using Native American languages for secret communication.

That got Johnston thinking about one particular group of Native Americans: the Navajos. Johnston knew more about the Navajos than just about any other white person in the United States. His parents, William and Margaret Johnston, had been Protestant missionaries to the Navajo for many years. Philip had spent most of his childhood among the Navajos. During that time, Navajo children were his only friends.

Having lived with the Navajo language from the age of four, Johnston was one of the few whites who could speak it fluently. At an early age, he served as translator for his parents and for other visiting whites. By the age of nine,

he had traveled to Washington, D.C., to translate for a
Navajo delegation that asked President Theodore Roosevelt to look into the government's treatment of the Navajos and their neighbors, the Hopi.

Johnston knew that the Navajo language is virtually im-
possible for an adult to master. Every syllable in the Navajo
language means something and must be pronounced cor-
rectly. Subtle differences in the tone can completely change
the meaning of a sentence. The Navajos use four separate
tones of voice: low, high, rising, and falling. The Navajo
words for "medicine" and "mouth," for example, have the
same pronunciation but are said with different tones.

The language is made even more difficult for outsiders
because of the precise way in which one object relates to
another. These complex relationships may seem trivial to
an outsider but are extremely important to the Navajos.
For example, Navajos have not one but several words
meaning "dropped." Which one a speaker chooses depends
on what object has been dropped. One word applies to
dropping a round object, and another word applies to
dropping a stick.

The Navajo language also reflects a view of the world
quite different from that of most other cultures. The Navajo view of life is that everything that they do and that
happens to them is related to the world around them. For
example, a Navajo would not say, "I am hungry." He or she
would say, "Hunger is hurting me."

Johnston had learned something about the military and
its need for rapid, secret communication while serving in
France during World War I. The more he looked into it, the

more he realized how ideal the Navajo language was for sending secret messages. He contacted officers at the U.S. Marines' Camp Elliott in southern California with his idea of creating a military code based on the Navajo language.

Lieutenant Colonel James Jones, a signal officer, met with Johnston in February 1942. At first, Johnston was greeted with skepticism. His notion was nothing new. Over the years, many armies had tried sending messages using obscure or ancient languages, including Native American languages. Back in World War I, Company D of the 141st Infantry had used eight Choctaw Indians to send and translate orders by telephone. The experiment had worked well enough on a limited basis against the Germans that the U.S. military continued to recruit Oneidas, Chippewas, Sac & Fox, and Commanches for signal corp work at the start of World War II. But Indian communications were not likely to be useful to the military on a large scale in the future. In the years between the wars, many German students had come to the United States to study Native Americans. The army guessed that the Germans had a good understanding of most Native American languages and could easily share that information with their allies in Japan.

The Germans had not, however, penetrated the Navajo tribe. The Navajo were so isolated, and their language so difficult, that in 1940 probably fewer than thirty people outside the Navajo tribe knew their language. Johnston pointed out that knowledge of other Native American languages would be of no help to the enemy in understanding Navajo. Navajo was as foreign to other tribes as it was to anyone else. Furthermore, it was strictly a spoken language. It had never been reduced to a written form that could be studied from afar.

Johnston pointed out the key difference between his plan and other attempts to use Native Americans for communication: He was not talking about simple translation of military orders into the Navajo language. He was talking about a *code* developed from Navajo.

Again, this was not earth-shattering news to the military. During World War I, the Canadians had tried to develop a code based on Indian languages. The plan had failed because Indian languages did not match up well with Western military terminology. The military had too many terms for which there was no Indian equivalent. There were also problems in finding enough Native Americans for a large-scale program. In 1941, the more than 180 Native American tribes had a total population of approximately 360,000. Most tribes numbered a few thousand at best. Out of these small numbers, even fewer were men of military age who could speak both their native language and English.

Again, Johnston argued that the Navajo-language situation was different. Navajo was unusually flexible and adaptable. While virtually all languages borrow terms from other languages to name new objects or concepts, the Navajos rarely needed to borrow a word. When the Spanish introduced the horse into the area, the Navajos developed their own word for this new creature. The same occurred with objects such as the automobile and airplane. The Navajos invented their own words, either by combining existing Navajo words or by creating totally new words.

The Navajos could also provide far more translators than any other tribe. At the time of the United States entry into World War II, there were roughly 55,000 Navajos, more than twice as many as in the next largest Native American group, the Sioux. Those numbers should be large enough, Johnston thought, to provide an ample corps of messengers.

Johnston spoke a few Navajo phrases to give the marines an idea of the complexity of the Navajo language. By this time he had sparked some interest. In March 1942, he was allowed to present a demonstration to an audience that included Major General Clayton Vogel (James Jones's superior officer) and Colonel Wethered Woodward from marine headquarters in Washington, D.C. Johnston was able to gain the cooperation of four Navajos living in the Los Angeles area and a Navajo soldier serving with the navy near San Diego. The Navajos were split into separate rooms. Military messages were given to one of the Navajos, who then translated the message into the Navajo language. This message was sent on to the second Navajo, who then translated the message back into English.

General Vogel was so impressed with the speed and accuracy of the translations that he requested authorization to proceed with Johnston's project. In February 1942, just two months after the Pearl Harbor attack, Philip Johnston was asked to prepare a proposal for organizing and using the Navajo code talkers.

Even with Colonel Woodward's endorsement, Vogel's request met with resistance at high-level command. The program was approved but scaled back drastically. Vogel's superiors were not ready to turn over such a crucial element of their communications system to a civilian and hundreds of untested Navajos. The marines chopped Johnston's proposed full-scale, two-hundred-man unit down to a thirty-man pilot program. That way, if the whole thing proved disastrous and the program had to be scrapped, the marines would not have invested much.

Philip Johnston was convinced that it would not take long before the Navajos proved their worth. He accepted the challenge of organizing the 382nd Platoon of the U.S. Marines for the pilot program. In April 1942, marine recruiters were dispatched to the Navajo reservation to find the first candidates.

► 3 ◄

Creating the Code

MARINE RECRUITERS WHO ENTERED Navajo territory might have thought they had wandered into a foreign land. The reservation was large enough to be a country unto itself. The boundaries encompassed more than 25,000 square miles of arid and semi-desert land, making it larger than the entire state of West Virginia.

The recruiters discovered that of all the Native American tribes, none was more determined than the Navajos to survive as a tribe. Few Navajos ever left the reservation. Few had any contact at all with the *belegaana*, as they called those of European extraction. Most Navajos held closely to their religious rituals, and they governed themselves according to the traditions of their clans. Although they willingly fought in the U.S. armed forces to protect the country against enemies, they did not forget the lesson of the Long Walk. The Navajos trusted neither the *belegaana* nor their government.

The worst effects of this mistrust showed in the educa-

A Navajo family in front of a traditional one-room hogan.

tion of young Navajos. According to the terms of the 1868 treaty, the United States agreed to provide adequate school facilities and one teacher for every thirty students. The Navajos agreed to send their children to these government schools. Neither side honored the pact. Government schools were few and poorly equipped. Thousands of Navajo children were left with no chance for an education.

On the other hand, Navajo parents were partly at fault

(COURTESY OF NATIONAL ARCHIVES)

for the poor educational system. Many of them were suspicious of these government schools. They kept their children at home to help tend sheep or raise crops. As a result, few Navajos learned to speak English, and many of those who did seldom had a chance to practice it.

Their poor understanding of English proved humiliating to many of the young men who volunteered to join the armed forces. According to Selective Service records from

25

that era, almost three out of five male Navajos of military age did not speak English, and nearly nine out of ten were classified as illiterate. The U.S. military sent home all those who were unable to speak and understand English. The Navajos finally persuaded the War Department to set up a few all-Navajo training platoons for non-English-speaking men who wanted to fight. Once these soldiers learned military English, they were mixed in with regular regiments.

Knowing that they would have to target the most educated Navajos for the code-talker program, marine recruiters visited government boarding schools at Fort Defiance in Arizona and at Fort Wingate and Shiprock in New Mexico. Since the purpose of the code-talker program was to provide secret communications, recruiters did not want to advertise what they had in mind.

At first the Navajos would have nothing to do with this mysterious recruiting team. Sergeant Frank Shinn appealed to Navajo tribal council chairman Chee Dodge for help. After hearing an explanation of the program, Dodge sent out a call for recruits over shortwave radio. The next morning, the marine recruiters were greeted by a long line of applicants. Some of these Navajos were so eager to sign up that they lied about their age. Dean Wilson was only fifteen when he joined the marines, three years short of the required age. Carl Gorman altered his birth date for the opposite reason. At age thirty-six, he was too old to qualify. Several Navajos resorted to desperate measures to make the marines' weight requirement of 122 pounds. One of them started eating bunches of bananas. Another, when told he was 3 pounds under the limit, drank 4 pounds of water to make the weight.

Many of these Navajo volunteers understood little about the code-talker program beyond the fact that it was a special program run by the marines. According to one volunteer, "When we were recruited, we knew only that we were to be specialists of some kind, but did not know we would have anything to do with setting up codes."[4] Some of the candidates confused the word "marine" with "submarine" and thought they would be training for undersea duty.

The thirty candidates who were selected and left for basic training camp near San Diego were totally unprepared for what lay ahead. Most of them had lived all their lives out in sheepherding country and had never had contact with the rest of American society. The trainees had to adapt to everything from strange food to bunkhouses to mechanized equipment. Such concepts as competition, so deeply ingrained in American culture, were foreign to them. When boxing matches were organized among the troops, the Navajos did not see the point. Why would anyone fight for no reason? They fought in these bouts, but their halfhearted efforts bewildered their *belegaana* officers.

Perhaps the most drastic adjustment for the mild-mannered, unaggressive Navajos was military discipline. Marine training instructors traditionally took pride in showing no mercy to their charges. The rigors of boot camp were meant to be a jolt to the ordinary recruit's system — a shock treatment for instilling discipline. For the Navajos, the shock treatment must have been more like a lightning bolt. Navajo boys who had enjoyed a great deal of freedom living in wide-open country suddenly found themselves under the absolute control of hard-nosed, screaming *belegaana* sergeants who could order them about at will.

The Navajos were run through long hours of calisthenics, basic training drills, lectures, and tedious, routine assignments such as guard duty. There was nothing in Navajo society to prepare the trainees for the rigid schedule and the seemingly endless list of petty regulations that had to be followed. Some recruits rebelled at first and refused to put on military uniforms.

Yet for the most part, the Navajos took their officers' abuse in easy stride. In fact, the impossibility of riling up the Navajos for any reason drove the drill instructors to despair.

Once the Navajo trainees had learned to cope with their strange surroundings, the rest was relatively easy. That included the torturous physical training meant to toughen up new marine recruits. On long, exhausting predawn hikes in full equipment, sergeants barked at the recruits, "Anyone who is tired of walking can start running!"

The Navajos seemed unaware that they were even being challenged by the fitness program. They registered no surprise or anxiety or fear no matter how difficult the exercise. Years of living in a harsh environment without the comfort of modern conveniences had already toughened them. These were people who were used to going without food for several days and who thought nothing of bathing in the snow. Nor did the tedium and drudgery of endlessly repeating difficult assignments have any apparent effect on them. According to a wartime issue of *Headquarters Bulletin*, "Instructors could not think of any strenuous drill or forced marches too tough for the Navajo."[5] In his evaluation, one general wrote that, as far as survival training was concerned, "the Navajo are without peer."[6]

The code talkers enjoyed telling the story of one particular survival exercise in the desert. The Navajos and a group of *belegaana* marine recruits were ordered on a two-day march in the desert. Each would be given only one canteenful of water to last those two days. At nightfall after the first day, the Navajos sneaked off and tapped into some desert plants for water. The next day they continued on with their canteens still quite full. The *belegaana* marines, meanwhile, had emptied their canteens and were fainting of thirst. Unaware of what the Navajos had done, the *belegaana* could only conclude that the Navajos were superhuman creatures.

Following boot camp, the Navajos were sent to Camp Pendleton, also near San Diego, to learn the techniques of communicating messages. The trainees studied Morse code, semaphore signals, techniques of military message-writing, wire laying, pole climbing, and communication procedures, and were trained in the operation of the radios that would be used in combat zones. Although most of them had no experience in electronics, the Navajos had to learn how to take apart and put together these bulky field radios and how to care for them so that they would not break or malfunction.

The most important task of all for the first group of

Navajos was to develop their code. First, they had to learn page after page of military terminology from all branches of the service. Then they were given 211 of the terms most likely to be used in the field. Their mission was to create a Navajo equivalent for each of these words. The code words had to be chosen with care. In order to maintain top secrecy, the marines would not allow any written version of the code out in the battle zones. Everything would have to be committed to memory.

The code talkers followed four basic rules in creating code words. First, the code words had to have some logical connection with the terms for which they stood. This was necessary to make memorization easier. Second, memorization would be far easier if the code words were unusu-

Eighteen-year-old cousins Preston Toledo (left) and Frank Toledo train for their assignment with a marine artillery unit. (Courtesy of National Archives)

ally descriptive or creative. Third, since time was crucial in many military operations, the code words had to be relatively short. Fourth, because accuracy was essential, the code talkers needed to avoid words that might be confused with other, similar words. This meant paying careful attention to what would happen if the proper Navajo tone or inflection could not be distinguished because of a fuzzy radio connection.

The task of thinking up code words that fit all the requirements was a mind-numbing struggle. Gradually, though, the Navajo code took shape. Names for different marine corps units were taken from the various clans to which each Navajo belonged. For example, "To dich ii nii" ("Bitter Water People") would refer to one unit, "Atsosi dine's" ("Feather People") to another.

Some of the code words were fairly straightforward. Airplanes were given names having to do with the other inhabitants of the sky—birds. Dive bombers acted much like sparrow hawks, and so the Navajo code word for dive bomber was *gini*, their word for sparrow hawk. The bombs delivered from these airplanes resembled the eggs delivered from birds. So the code word for bombs was *a-ye-shi*, which meant eggs.

The American terms for ground forces attacking from the sea was "amphibious assault" ("amphibious" means able to cope on both dry land and water). The Navajos chose an amphibian, the frog (*chat* in the Navajo language), to represent this type of action.

Some of the code words reflected the Navajo worldview. The Navajo family is dominated by the mother's side of the family, so the code talkers chose the word *ne-he-mah*, which means "our mother," as their symbol for the United States. Other code words painted vivid pictures of the terms they represented. "January," for example, was *yas-nil-tes*, which means "crusted snow." "Route" became *gah-bih-tkeen*, or "rabbit trail."

Other code words reflected the Navajo sense of humor. The army, which was the Marine Corps' rival in the U.S. armed forces, became *lei-cha-ih-yil-knee-ih*, which means "dog-faces." This was a name that Native Americans had often used for *belegaana* soldiers during the Indian Wars. The Navajos used a word meaning "gun that squats" to indicate a mortar. The translation of their word for bombardment was "iron rain."

Despite their best efforts, the Navajos were unable to come up with a code word for every military term. Some of the verbs, particularly, were difficult to translate. For a very few of these, they simply used the Navajo term: *al-tah-je-jay* for "attack"; *nal-dzil* for "reinforce."

In order to include more words in their operations than just the 211 assigned terms, the code talkers added an alphabet code. They simply took the English letter, thought of something that started with that letter, and then used the Navajo word for that object. For the letter "A," they chose the ant, which in Navajo is *wol-la-chee*, The letter "B" was represented by the Navajo word for "bear," which is *shush*. The letter "C" could be transmitted by saying "*moasi*," the Navajo word for "cat."

This alphabet was especially useful in communicating locations. For example, if a code talker was transmitting orders to attack the island of Saipan, he could say, "Al-tah-je-jay dsibeh wol-la-chee tkin bi-sodih wol-la-chee nesh-chee." The code talker receiving the message would translate this message as "Attack sheep ant ice pig ant nut." He would recognize the alphabet words and would spell out "Saipan," using the first letters of each of the English words.

The code talkers were trained in a concentrated four-week course containing 176 hours of basic training. This did not include time they had to spend studying and practicing so that they could instantly transmit messages from English to Navajo code. There was no room for error. The slightest mistake in sending or receiving a message could cause the deaths of hundreds of marines or could ruin months of meticulous planning. As an extra incentive to the trainees, the Navajos were promised that they would be promoted to the rank of private first class at the end of training. Normally, newly enlisted men had to serve a year before receiving the promotion, which meant, among other things, a pay increase.

During the final two weeks of training, the Navajos were put into simulated battle situations with their radios. Marine officers tried every possible way of breaking the Navajo code. Intelligence experts recorded the Navajo messages and took them back to their offices to decipher. According to one experienced code-cracker, "It sounded like gibberish. We couldn't even transcribe it, much less crack it."[7]

Navajo soldiers who were not in the code-talker program listened in on the communications. They could not

Peter Nahaidinao (left) and Joseph Gatewood plan their
course of action in night exercises at an Amphibious Scout
School intelligence program under the supervision of Corporal
Lloyd Oliver. (COURTESY OF NATIONAL ARCHIVES)

make sense of the messages, either. Yet the messages were
received and translated by other code talkers without error.

One week before completing the course, disappointing
news reached the Navajo trainees. Officers high up in the
marine chain of command had overridden the previous orders about promotion. The trainees would *not* be moved
up in rank as they had been promised. For the descendants
of the people of the Long Walk, this reversal could hardly
have eased their distrust of the U.S. government. Yet they
accepted the situation without complaint. Of the thirty
who started the program, twenty-nine completed it.

Philip Johnston's program had proven a great success.
Orders were given to expand it. Although he was techni-

cally too old to qualify, Johnston was accepted into the U.S. Marines and placed in charge of the code-talker training program.

Two of the trainees, John Benally and Johnny Manuelito, were assigned to return to the Navajo reservation to recruit new volunteers. The shortage of young Navajo men with a good command of English made this a difficult task. Many men eager to join this select, secret program were turned away. As before, some Navajos who did not qualify because of their age slipped through the screening process. Code talkers were even recruited from among those who had already enlisted in other branches of the armed forces, and a few were simply reassigned into the code-talker program. By the end of the war, about 450 Navajos had been recruited for code-talker training. Of that number, only 30 failed to complete the demanding course.

Several of the original code talkers were retained as instructors at the training camp. The remainder were sent off to the South Pacific for their first assignment. Each wave of new Navajo trainees would be rushed over to join them. Although the recruits had been eager to join the code talkers and serve in the armed forces, none could have realized what they were about to get into.

The United States, still unable to match the military strength of the Japanese, had been pushed back throughout the Pacific. Until the European war against Nazi Germany was won, President Roosevelt planned simply to try to keep the Japanese advance from spreading too far. But U.S. military commanders in the Pacific were growing restless. Somehow the tide had to be turned before the Japanese owned every piece of land from China to Australia. If the Japanese gained control of the entire Pacific area, the task of trying to dislodge them would be overwhelming. The United States also needed to make a determined stand just to boost the country's morale in the face of repeated Japanese successes.

Until their superior industries could crank out enough military matériel to supply a major offensive, the United States and its allies could stop the Japanese advance only by concentrating all their forces in one area.

Their target was a small chain of islands known as the Solomons. In the early summer of 1942, Allied forces had observed a small force of Japanese building a runway on one of the largest of the Solomon Islands. An air base in the Solomons would extend Japanese air power even further into the Pacific. The Allied forces wanted to put a stop to this constant expansion. Although there was no hope that they could sustain an attack on most of Japan's new territory, they believed the Solomons were vulnerable. The islands lay at the very end of what had become a long Japanese supply line, and the Allies hoped that the enemy would find it difficult to transport reinforcements to the relatively sparse defenses on the Solomons.

The American commanders decided that their stand had to be made immediately. The plan for attacking the Solomon Islands was thrown together hurriedly. Even those assigned to plan and lead the campaign received fewer than five weeks' notice. Joining the expedition were thousands of untested American troops who thought they had been headed for New Zealand and Australia for six months of combat preparation. Because there was no time to order and gather all the desired equipment, American soldiers had to make do with poor substitutes. As a result, the plan was commonly criticized as Operation Shoestring.

Its success depended upon surprise. Since there seemed to be no way to pass information along without its reaching enemy ears, the U.S. command clammed up. Most of the landing force that assembled in the waters off the northeast coast of Australia did not know the name of their destination. Few of them would have been able to locate the place even if they heard the name. But the name was one that would soon be imprinted in the memories of most Americans: Guadalcanal. The code talkers would be joining this critical campaign in progress.

► 4 ◄

Earning Trust

THE MARINES HUDDLED, GRIMLY silent, as their transport ship slowly floated them in toward the beaches of
Guadalcanal. Each rolling wave brought the marines closer
to the edge of their protective escort of planes and naval
artillery. With each passing second they drew closer to the
loaded muzzles of an enemy who had never been defeated
in a ground engagement.

To their relief those hidden guns remained silent when
the marines landed on the shore. The sparse Japanese
forces on Guadalcanal had been chased into the hills by
the American bombardment. The marines made no contact with the defenders during the first day, and quickly
took over the abandoned airstrip.

Yet the suspicions of peril lingered. No one who saw the
traffic jam on the beaches of Guadalcanal could have much
confidence in the operation. The Americans were overwhelmed by the task of landing and distributing supplies
for 19,000 marines. Tons of equipment piled up on the

sand, while vessels waited offshore for space to clear so they could land more supplies.

Then the Japanese planes arrived. Japanese bombers and fighters swarmed over the area, dropping their deadly loads. When word came that the Japanese navy had crushed an Allied naval squadron, American commanders decided it was no longer safe for their ships to linger in the area. The American support fleet withdrew, taking with them great quantities of crucial unloaded supplies, such as artillery, bulldozers, and food.

The marines watched the disappearance of the ships with horror. They were stranded without air or naval support in the middle of a sea controlled by the Japanese navy. For the present, they could hope for no supplies other than what they had carried ashore with them, and that included a mere thirty-seven-day supply of food.

Some of the marines believed they had been left to die. They were trapped on an island with a resourceful, well-prepared, and fanatically courageous enemy whom they could not see. "I was never so scared in my entire life," admitted Jimmy Begay, one of the first code talkers to see action.[8]

In this dense tropical forest, the marines could not count on aerial scouting reports to outline enemy positions. For the most part, the two armies would be stalking each other through mucky bogs, seven-foot-high blades of coarse, skin-ripping grass, steep ridges, and nearly impassable jungle.

As the marines groped through this wilderness, suddenly cut loose to fend for themselves, the radios became

The view from the ground as a marine cautiously advances through rough terrain toward an unseen enemy. (COURTESY OF NATIONAL ARCHIVES)

as important to them as their weapons. The radio was their only link with the command and support elements of their forces. As various patrols branched out to probe the dense terrain around them, the radio lines were the thin thread that held them together. Without some kind of reliable communication system, they could easily be split up and scattered through the Guadalcanal jungle as they tried to repel the furious assaults of the Japanese.

These marines were in close contact with an enemy who could easily monitor their communications. It was exactly the kind of situation for which the Navajo code talkers had been organized. The code talkers sent in to Guadalcanal were split up among the patrols. On one of the first nights after they had fanned out into the island's interior, one Navajo sent a coded message to another.

That message had a frightening impact, one that Philip Johnston had not anticipated. While the Navajo operator was still talking, his strange speech hit several marine detachments like a smoking grenade. The marine command had been tight-lipped about the whole Navajo code-talker program, so few of the men in the field knew anything about it. All they knew was that people were speaking a foreign language on American military radios—and for all the marines knew, that language was Japanese.

People in extreme danger who are not informed about what is happening around them are dry kindling for the rapid spread of rumors. Before long the marine camp was ablaze in scuttlebutt (the soldier's term for unconfirmed reports). The Japanese were using American radios! The only way they could have taken control of American radios was to have captured them from marines. Since the Japanese were transmitting on several radios, that meant they must have overrun the marine positions. Maybe they had destroyed most of the expedition, or surrounded the marines, or cut them off from the beaches.

When the officers had restored order and figured out what was causing all the ruckus, they were in no mood to listen to the benefits of the Navajo code system. The Navajos were directed to stop sending messages before they threw the entire command into panic.

This was not the only time Navajo messages sent bewildered Americans scurrying for cover. Some months later, a navy warship was charging at full speed toward the Marshall Islands, where a major sea battle was shaping up. The Americans, counting on the element of surprise, were operating under a veil of silence. As the warship neared the action, its radio operators broke silence and sent out a message in Navajo code.

A radio operator on one of the American ships heard the Navajo message come in loud and clear. Again, he could only assume its language was Japanese. The volume was so loud that it convinced him his ship had run right into the middle of a Japanese fleet.

Since secure lines of communication often hold the balance of life and death for fighting men, officers are not inclined to take chances with them. Some of those who had had Navajos assigned to their commands viewed the whole code-talking plan as an impractical scheme cooked up by some dreamer sitting at a desk back in the States, someone ignorant of combat conditions. A few episodes such as those on Guadalcanal and at the Marshall Islands were all it took to convince them that their instincts had been right.

Not only did the Navajos *sound* like the Japanese to many marines, they also *looked* like them. There was no one "type" of Navajo that could be immediately recognized. Navajo men can display great differences in size, build, skin color, and facial appearance. They do, however, tend toward a number of characteristics that are more similar to the Japanese than to the *belegaana:* dark hair, dark skin, sparse facial hair, high cheekbones, occasionally even Asian-appearing eyes.

Under the stress of war, marines not familiar with Native Americans might have mistaken Corporal Lloyd Oliver's dark hair and skin for the features of a Japanese infiltrator. (COURTESY OF NATIONAL ARCHIVES)

Even marines who under normal circumstances would have no difficulty in distinguishing a Navajo from a Japanese could easily make a mistake in the heat of close battle. When a soldier suddenly poked through the cane fields, a marine did not have time to carefully study his appearance. A half-second delay could mean the difference between life and death. This put the Navajos in an extremely perilous situation in the dense forests and craggy ravines of the Pacific. They were further at risk because of the Japanese soldier's intense devotion to duty. Even a Japanese who was cornered and faced hopeless odds was far more likely to fight to the death than to surrender. Because of this, American soldiers kept their fingers close to their triggers.

The problem was even worse when the marines joined with army units in the battlefield. While most marines had quickly become aware of the Navajos, the army was totally in the dark. Many of the Navajos had close encounters with U.S. Army soldiers, who were especially enraged at the thought of enemy soldiers skulking around in American uniforms.

Most of these incidents resulted in nothing more than inconvenience, both for the Navajo and for the command post. One Navajo code talker tried frantically to get a message through to another unit on the front lines. No matter how many times he tried, there was no answer. Concern and confusion reigned over what had happened to this unit. Finally it was discovered that the Navajo who was to receive the message had been captured by his fellow marines and was being held prisoner.

Sometimes the result was merely comical. During heavy fighting on one of the islands, a group of marines captured a small pocket of Japanese prisoners. One of the Navajos was assigned to take the prisoners back to the American command post. The Japanese marched in single file while the Navajo trailed behind, covering them with his rifle. When the procession arrived at the American camp, the *belegaana* marines viewing the spectacle howled with laughter. It looked for all the world as though an armed Japanese was herding unarmed Japanese into the American camp! "Which ones are the prisoners?" they teased.

For other Navajos, the mistaken identity was far from a laughing matter. One code talker, who was further disadvantaged by having a wispy beard under his chin that looked very much like the beards worn by many Japanese, ran into a string of trouble. He got lost behind his own lines and was captured by an American guard. After talking his way out of that mess, he was immediately captured by another American squad. Since the Navajo was dressed in American uniform, he was considered a spy behind American lines, and there was some debate about what to do with him. Spies could be shot. The Navajo managed to get transported back to headquarters before any action was taken against him. There he was identified by another Navajo and finally set free.

After several close calls, many of the marine units assigned a *belegaana* bodyguard to protect their code talkers from confused Americans. Even this did not completely guarantee the Navajos' safety. Late in the war, a code talker chose the wrong time to poke his head out of a cave. American soldiers standing outside took aim at him and would have shot him down had not the code talker's *belegaana* buddy, who was in the cave with him, rushed to the rescue.

The confusion caused by the presence of Navajo code talkers added to marine officers' suspicions of the program. One officer declared that the code talkers were "more trouble than they were worth."[9] A few marine officers refused to use code talkers at all. Other officers did not understand their purpose. They used the Navajos as runners to carry messages from the front through enemy lines. As a result, some code talkers were assigned to regular marine duty. Others were given special tasks. A number of code talkers were killed while serving as message runners.

Most of the commanders, though, while skeptical of the Navajo code, kept an open mind. One colonel agreed to use the Navajos only if they could prove they were better than his current communication method. The colonel was using a system known as the "white code." The white code involved a mechanical device that used a revolving cylinder to translate a message into a code. This ciphered message was then sent over the radio and deciphered by the receiver.

A simple contest was set up in the field, pitting two Navajo code talkers against two marines using the white-code system. Both teams would be given a message to send on one end and a response to send back from the other end. Whichever method produced an accurately translated response first would be the communication method of choice.

Four and a half minutes later, the Navajo team completed an accurate transmission of the message. The white-code team was still trying to piece together their encoded message, far from completion. Because the need for secret, quick communication was so essential to the marines, tests such as this were repeated often in the South Pacific.

The code-talking system as it was first set up did contain flaws, and no one knew this better than the Navajos who used it. The 211-word vocabulary that had seemed enormous when they had devised and memorized code words back in training now proved to be inadequate for the job. New pieces of equipment were being developed all the time. Bazookas (hand-held rocket launchers), sniper-scopes (special eyewear that allowed soldiers to see objects in the dark), and various types of troop-carrying seacraft were brought into action. New tactics, strategies, and terminology came into use, prompted by the development of amphibious warfare. The Navajo code was not equipped to take these into account. Messages were getting bogged down by all the words the Navajos had to spell to make up for their limited vocabulary.

Not only was this extra reliance on spelling time-consuming and more subject to human error, it was always dangerous. The more spelling the code talkers did, the more the Japanese could make use of frequency charts to decode the messages. Even though the code talkers used Navajo words for the English letters, these words still occurred with the normal frequency found in English words. It would not take long before the Japanese figured out that *wol-la-chee* was a vowel. From there it would be a simple matter to determine that it stood for the letter "A."

These concerns were relayed to code-talker training headquarters back in California. Responding quickly to the problem, the Navajo code supervisors expanded their vocabulary to nearly double its original size.

Code talkers also added alternate Navajo words for some of the more commonly used English letters. To simplify memorization, these alternate Navajo words, like the orig-

47

inals, translated English terms that began with the desired letter. For example, "A" could be transmitted by saying either *be-las-saaa* (Navajo for "apple") or *tse-nihl* ("ax"), as well as *wol-la-chee* ("ant"). Six of the most commonly used English letters (E, T, A, I, O, N) were given two substitutes. Six others (S, H, R, D, L, U) were given one substitute. By interchanging alternate code words with the originals, the Navajo could disrupt the normal pattern of frequency.

While the marines were learning to work with the code talkers, the brutal struggle for control of Guadalcanal raged on through the fall and into the winter of 1942. Fierce naval battles raged in the surrounding seas as the United States and Japan maneuvered for mastery of the shipping lanes. Thousands of Japanese soldiers were ferried to Guadalcanal to push back the Americans. The United States threw in reinforcements of its own, including warplanes that could operate from the runway, which the marines now controlled.

Japan's desperate, reckless attacks were driven back repeatedly. The Japanese brought in heavy artillery to finish off the job, but were thwarted by steady, pounding rains that turned the island into a truck-eating quagmire. During one major engagement, the forces of nature wiped out technology on both sides. Japan could not move its heavy guns into place; the United States could not launch its aircraft from the soupy runway. The Americans held on doggedly to their positions. By the new year, the Japanese were finally forced to abandon the island.

During the Guadalcanal action, the Navajo code talkers were not able to make believers of everyone. The frequency with which they were used continued to depend primarily on individual commanders. Some officers held out against the code-talker system until later in the war. But the efforts of the code talkers were noticed by Major General Alexander Vandegrift, the leader of the American expedition in Guadalcanal. In December 1942, when his forces finally wrested control of the island from the Japanese, General Vandegrift put in a request for eighty-three more Navajo code talkers for his division.

One of the most striking examples of the code talkers' value involved the Japanese stronghold at Rabaul, the key port in a cluster of islands northeast of Papua New Guinea that were under Australian protection. A wide harbor at the base of a ring of volcanoes provided a ready port for distributing supplies. The terrain surrounding the harbor was also ideal for airplane runways.

During the Japanese offensive of early 1942, Japanese forces overwhelmed a small garrison of Australian defenders and took over the town. They then cleared off land for an air base and made Rabaul their primary base for continued attacks to the south. Ships filled with weapons, ammunition, troops, combat gear, food, and other supplies poured into the harbor. Japanese planes taking off from Rabaul dropped bombs on New Guinea to the southwest, on the key Australian supply center of Port Moresby to the south, and on the Solomon Islands to the southeast. Rabaul housed the bombers that chased off the American fleet and left the marines on Guadalcanal without air and sea support. By the summer of 1942, Japanese forces anchored at Rabaul threatened to choke off the main supply lines from the United States to Australia and New Zealand.

The American and Allied forces desperately wanted to knock out this Japanese stronghold, but the harbor was well protected by anti-aircraft guns. Unless American planes could sneak in undetected, there was little chance of inflicting any damage.

But a successful sneak attack was unlikely: The Japanese were reading American naval orders right along with the American pilots. Because they could easily break the navy codes, the Japanese defenders on Rabaul generally received plenty of advance warning when an attack was coming. American pilots trying to bomb the base flew into a sky lit up by flames of death from the guns of the well-prepared

Pilot's view of the Allied raid on Rabaul harbor. Fleeing Japanese warships can be seen ahead of the white tails of their wakes. (COURTESY OF NATIONAL ARCHIVES)

defenses. So many planes were shot down over Rabaul that American pilots renamed the place Dead End.

In order to stem the flood of information into enemy hands, eleven Navajo code talkers were sent in to take charge of navy air communications. Instantly the Japanese on Rabaul fell into a cloud of uncertainty. On November 5, 1943, American planes launched from aircraft carriers evaded Japanese spotters and caught the base defenders unawares. In a flurry of bombing runs, they hit Japanese ships, planes, and storage facilities. Six days later another wave of U.S. bombers roared in unannounced. Rather than remain exposed to such murderous attacks, the Japanese fleet fled the harbor. Although Rabaul was not actually re-taken until much later in the war, the base no longer played a role in aiding Japan's forces.

The Navajos also provided key links between ground forces and naval and air support as the United States and its allies moved to secure their hold on the Solomons. The Allies began a drive through Bougainville, the northern-most of the six largest Solomons, in November 1943. By mid-1944, they had secured all of the Solomons. With this victory, the U.S. forces broke the Japanese momentum and bought time for the campaigns that were to follow.

▶ 5 ◀

Life in the War Zone

IF INITIATION INTO THE *belegaana* world of boot camp had seemed a bizarre dream to the sheltered Navajos, it was a cozy, warm coccoon compared with the South Pacific nightmare into which they sailed. Training camp had been just a few hundred miles off the reservation, and they had lived among a group of fellow Navajos. In the Pacific war, they were dispersed among various groups of marines. As if the pressures of life-threatening combat in a foreign environment thousands of miles from home were not enough stress, the Navajos bore the added burden of living among the *belegaana*, under *belegaana* rules.

Navajo culture assumed that the *Dineh* ("the People"), as the Navajos called themselves, had no choice but to follow a narrow path through a world swarming with supernatural beings. Powerless creatures such as humans could survive only by learning to live in harmony with these forces. This was accomplished by following the many ancient Navajo traditions that governed how a person was to act toward others and toward nature. These customs emerged from a worldview completely different from that of the *belegaana*. Those who knew the Navajo best feared that these customs were bound to clash with the realities of life among U.S. Marines in the South Pacific.

Navajos were taught that they must never step over another person. Even in their traditional one-room hogans, great care was taken to avoid stepping over sleeping family members. How would such a rule fare in crowded tents and foxholes, among marines who were unaware of any such custom?

Navajos were taught not to kill snakes. Was that practical or even possible in some of the snake-infested hellholes the marines found themselves in? How would the Navajos react to a *belegaana* slashing a snake in half out of fear or simply for the fun or it? Navajos were taught never to eat a piece of food with the point of a knife stuck in it. Would this cause problems at mealtime? Navajos took great care to avoid having beasts cross their paths and to stay away from any tree damaged by lightning. Would these traditional taboos clash with orders from a superior officer to take up a certain position?

Communication between the Navajo and *belegaana* marines was often limited because of their different societal attitudes. Sociologists believe that the unique Navajo culture is so distinctive that even the best interpreters cannot be confident that they are accurately conveying thoughts and feelings from one language to another.

The many cultural barriers between Navajo and *belegaana* marines did occasionally cause difficulties. During one of the island campaigns, a marine communications section was issued its rations. The packages were sent to the *belegaana* teletype operators, who were instructed to break up the ten-meal packages and distribute them among themselves and the Navajos. They followed these routine orders, only to discover that the Navajos refused to eat the meals.

After puzzling over the problem for a while, the *belegaana* marines concluded that the procedure had violated the Navajo sense of pride. The instruction that *belegaana* operators were to share their meals with the Navajos was taken by the Navajos to mean that the meals were intended for the *belegaana* and that the Navajos were being given the meals as charity. Navajo pride prohibited them from accepting.

Although this was not at all what was intended by the procedure, there was no way to convey the point to the Navajos. Headquarters finally solved the problem by reissuing the rations to the Navajos and instructing them to share with the other operators. The Navajos were quite willing to share, and the *belegaana*, who were more familiar with the supply system, did not consider it a matter of charity.

For the most part, however, Navajo and *belegaana* marines got along very well. The Navajos, who were raised to be tolerant of other peoples' behavior, were easy to be around. Most of them reported that they were treated well and made many *belegaana* friends during the war. Because of the tight blanket of secrecy muffling the code talkers, many of the *belegaana* marines had no idea why there were so many Navajos among them, or what these people were doing. But they accepted the fact that the Navajos were performing some special task that was aiding their cause.

Belegaana marines, as a whole, were more accepting of minorities than was society in general. Many, whose knowledge of Native Americans commonly came only from books or movies, seemed genuinely tickled to have a Navajo in their group. According to code talker William Kien, "They were willing to fight and work with me. Some even took pictures of me and them to take home. They would write home, 'This is an American Indian. He's with the message outfit.' "[10]

The Navajo trait that posed the most difficult problem for code talkers in the Pacific was the fear of death. This did not mean that the Navajos were unusually afraid of dying. Rather, they wanted no part of anything that had already died. The Navajo faith, like many religions, taught that people are not totally extinguished at their deaths. Unlike religions such as Christianity, however, the traditional Navajo religion did not assign the souls of the dead to an afterlife in another world. Traditional Navajos believed that only the evil part of a dead creature or person lingered on Earth. The *chindi*, as these spirits were called, returned to the place of their dying to terrorize the living. *Chindi* were to be avoided at all costs.

Because of their fear and hatred of *chindi*, Navajos deliberately avoided anything remotely connected with death. Once a person was dead, his or her name was not to be mentioned again, even if the dead person was a loved one.

If a person died in his or her hogan, the body had to be taken out through a hole in the northern wall, north being the direction of evil. In most cases, the hogan was burned to the ground. One of the greatest favors a *belegaana* could offer to Navajos was to bury their dead relatives for them. Burial was an ominous task, with elaborate ritual precautions taken to protect those who had to perform it. The Navajos' fear of spirits of death was so powerful that many did not even like to look at the bodies of dead animals.

In the Pacific war, the Navajo code talkers were surrounded by *chindi*, more *chindi* than they could have imagined in their worst fears. They lived among death and slept among death. Bodies of dying and dead comrades had to be pulled out of slimy rivers and vine-choked ditches. Navajos on the front lines huddled in their foxholes all night long while dead enemies lay in the darkness around them.

Yet even this unsettling closeness with their worst fear did not deter the Navajo code talkers from carrying out their duties. One code talker reported: "One night a screaming Japanese soldier leaped into the trench and killed my partner with a samurai sword before other marines could shoot him. I had to stay there sending messages with my friend's blood gushing over me."[11]

The Navajos showed a great ability to accept circumstances beyond their control. As much as they feared the *chindi*, there was no escape from the dead. Death was a fact of life in the Pacific war. Survival instincts were stronger even than the fear of all traditional taboos, and so the Navajos simply learned to live with their situation.

A key source of their ability to stay calm in the midst of terror and anxiety was the Navajos' religious beliefs. Navajos believed that their health depended upon three people: the medical doctor; the diagnostician, or person who discovered how the patient's mind and body were in disharmony with the world; and the singer, who performed elaborate rituals that restored the patient to health.

Doctors were considered the least important of the healers, providing only temporary relief or repair. The diagnostician was more important because he could find the deeper problem underlying the sickness. But the singer was the one who could actually put the patient and his world back in balance.

The singer was the central figure in traditional rituals, many of which had been performed for code talkers before they left the reservation. The two most important of these ceremonies were the Blessing Way and the Enemy Way.

The Blessing Way, which was invoked in crisis situations to bring good hope and well-being, involved several days of singing and ceremony. The singing retold the story of the creation of human life on Earth and how people were taught to live in peace and harmony with nature. It was usually performed in emergency situations, to restore health.

The Enemy Way was especially important in bolstering the Navajo warriors against the aura of death that surrounded them. The ceremony often included a sand painting that could take fifteen men an entire day to complete. The Enemy Way was meant to protect soldiers from "ghost sickness" caused by the spirits of the enemies whom they

Navajo patient sits by a sand painting during a Blessing Way ceremony. The person on his left wears a ceremonial mask as part of the healing ceremony. (PHOTOGRAPH BY SIMEON SCHWEMBERGER, COURTESY OF THE LIBRARY OF CONGRESS)

killed. Although the code talkers were trained more for communications than for actual combat, they also performed regular marine duties, and the Enemy Way ceremony was immensely reassuring to them.

The servicemen did not have to be present at the Enemy Way ceremony in order to receive its blessing. In May 1944, relatives on the reservation held a combined Enemy Way rite for 150 Navajos stationed in the Pacific. For this particular ceremony, photographs of the soldiers were gathered and laid out in front of the Enemy Way singer. Christian Navajos were invited to add their songs and their prayers to the traditional Enemy Way ceremony, which went on through the night.

The Navajo community tried to contribute in other ways

to the safe return of their soldiers. Throughout the war, many of them planted prayer feathers, decorated with turquoise, in the ground to help protect the servicemen.

Typical of the Navajos was William Kien, who was given a Blessing Way ceremony and a special medicine by his uncle. The uncle assured the young man that he would return home safely. Although Kien was thrown into vicious fighting in the Marshall Islands and was eighty percent disabled by his wounds, he returned home as he expected.

The Navajos did not leave all religious ceremony to the home front, either. Most of them carried buckskin pouches stuffed with corn pollen as protection. Some of them also carried a small bag of medicine prepared from the gallbladders of bears, skunks, eagles, and mountain lions, medicine formulated to protect Navajos who walked among strangers. One of the code talkers reported that he never sent a message out without asking the spirits to help him do his job effectively. Navajo Christians offered prayers of a different variety.

In addition to the adjustments the Navajos had to make to fighting a war under *belegaana* authority, they faced the same hardships that confronted all servicemen in the Pacific. Few Americans, Navajo or otherwise, had any experience with the steamy, rain-soaked islands of the South Pacific.

Soldiers serving in the Pacific had to endure some of the most wretched living conditions imaginable. They had to hack their way through dense jungles choked with slippery, rotting vegetation. They had to slog through slimy, stinking bogs that came up to their waists, plagued by hordes of malaria-carrying mosquitoes and other, enormous insects. Dripping with sweat from the stifling heat and humidity, they pushed through tall grasses up to their eyes, and trudged up steep ridges while carrying packs that weighed over 100 pounds.

Radio operators had it no easier than anyone else. In the age before transistors and microchips, most of the radio units weighed a good 80 pounds. The units were usually hooked to a tree and took two men to operate—one to crank up the electrical power, one to transmit. Since front lines rarely remained stationary in the Pacific war, radio operators were constantly lugging their equipment from place to place while bullets whistled around them.

Some Pacific battles were fought in jungles that received as much as 200 inches of rain a year. The troops often fought, and sent messages, in torrential rains that turned many of their camps into oozing rivers of mud. The ocean waters around them were filled with sharks, the rivers with leeches and crocodiles. Jungles teemed with snakes and man-made hazards such as booby traps.

U.S. troops could not always depend on full stocks of food and other supplies. Small groups or individuals could easily be cut off from their main camps and forced to fend for themselves. Living in close quarters without proper sanitation, troops were especially prone to diseases such as dysentery.

The Navajo code talkers, however, were the descendants of those who had survived the Long Walk. They were not strangers to harsh conditions and meager supplies, and

*Corporal Henry Blake, Jr., and Private First Class George Kirk
had to hack out this clearing in the dense jungle near the
Bougainville front lines before sending their message.* (COURTESY
OF NATIONAL ARCHIVES)

they knew how to endure difficult situations. Although the South Pacific climate and terrain were a far cry from the dry, open lands of the southwestern United States, the Navajos were able to adapt. They did not find hardships as difficult to bear as those more used to modern luxuries did. Most of the Navajos never missed having modern conveniences such as running water and electricity, because such things had never been available to them. Except for the ability to fight off disease, the Navajos were better suited to coping with this brutal life than many of their *belegaana* counterparts.

When supplies ran tight or supply lines were cut off, the marines often had to go without food. While this was undoubtedly a new and uncomfortable experience for many, it was nothing new to the Navajos. Living as they had in fairly unproductive lands, they were used to the sight of bare cupboards. Many of them had spent a good deal of time out in the open country with few provisions until they returned home. In the 1930s, the U.S. Department of the Interior had determined that Navajo sheep were overgrazing the land and ordered the Navajos to reduce their flocks by half. Many had never recovered from this devastating loss of livelihood and had lived in poverty since.

Having spent so little time inside houses, the Navajos were more used to scratching for some of the tidbits that nature had to offer. During frantic fighting in the dense jungles of Guadalcanal, one Navajo lieutenant was cut off from his own forces. Instead of surrendering or making a blind dash through the enemy lines to get back to his unit, the lieutenant lay low and bided his time. For seven days,

until he was able to locate the American forces, he survived by eating ants and snails.

On the island of Okinawa, in the final days of the war,
another group of Navajos found goats running loose in the
middle of the combat zone. Mutton and goat meat were
mainstays of the Navajo diet, but they were not common
items on the marine menu. The opportunity was too good
to pass up, and the Navajos decided to use their spare time
gathering their own rations. In the dark of night they
sneaked out of camp. The next day's supper turned into a
feast with choice cuts of goat.

In addition to learning to cope with a rugged, foreign
environment, the U.S. troops had to come to grips with the
unique nature of their enemy. Seldom had any army fought
with the tenacity and disregard for personal safety shown
by Japanese forces. The Japanese troops' pride and their
devotion to family and country were so great that they
could not bear to dishonor their cause by surrendering.
They had equal disdain for enemies who surrendered.
American forces knew that if they fell into enemy hands,
they could expect no mercy.

Japanese forces were relentless. Marines could never
rest; the Japanese might attack at any time. Cover of night
offered no relief from the day's fighting; it only made
matters worse. The Japanese often took advantage of the
darkness, when they could creep right into a marine camp
without being seen. A marine lying low in the forward
trenches sometimes tied a cord around his wrist, with the
other end tied to the wrist of a marine in a nearby trench.

During the night, each would occasionally tug on the cord to make sure his buddy was still alive.

The Japanese also had no qualms about fighting in the middle of a violent storm, in steady rain, or in the steamiest midday weather. They had been taught that the Americans were soft and used to luxury and would be too miserable to fight well under such conditions.

Japanese soldiers were skilled in the art of concealment. American soldiers never knew when a gun-toting enemy might pop up out of the brush or leap out of a hidden cave. A sniper might suddenly fire a shot from high in a palm tree. The bravery of Japanese soldiers was virtually limitless. They would try to swim around an American position to attack from the rear, and at times a cluster of them might roar out of the hills, screaming "Banzai!" or "Marine, you die!" in a suicide charge.

In many ways, the Navajos were well suited to confronting this type of enemy. Stealth, surprise, and close combat were all elements of traditional Navajo fighting. The Navajos' skill at walking noiselessly over the ground, in finding their way and keeping their bearings even in darkness, and in staying out of sight proved particularly useful against the Japanese. One marine sergeant reported, "They could crawl through the jungle without a sound and hide where there wasn't anywhere to hide."[12]

Navajo sergeant Frank Few's experience was hardly typical, but it did demonstrate the survival capacity of the Navajo. The sergeant's patrol was ambushed by Japanese soldiers. Few was stabbed by a bayonet before he made his escape. He then fought his way through a line of Japanese barring his path to the main group of marines.

After working so hard to get back to safety, Few was disheartened to see that he had not reached safety after all. The marines had been overwhelmed by the Japanese attack and forced to abandon their position. The wounded Few dove into the water and swam four and a half miles through shark-infested ocean to safety.

▶ 6 ◀

Breaking Japanese Codes

WHILE THE CONTRIBUTIONS OF the code talkers were vital to the Allied war effort in the Pacific, their work did not often provide the breathtaking drama of a daring infantry charge or a heroic stand against overwhelming odds. After all, the Navajo code was designed for the low-profile purpose of keeping communications flowing smoothly between the command post and the field.

A good code is like a well-crafted component of an automobile engine. The contributions of the individual engine parts are seldom appreciated until the car breaks down at a crucial time. In the same way, the code talkers' role consisted, for the most part, of reliably performing a routine job. The tremendous contribution of the Navajo code can best be understood by considering what happened to the Japanese when their codes broke down.

Japan's most important code failure occurred with its top-secret Purple Code. This code was produced by a cipher machine of a kind first developed shortly after World

War I. The Japanese version consisted of two electric type-writers wired to either end of a cipher box that contained a series of wheels, bars, and rotors. A letter typed on the first typewriter would send an electronic signal into the cipher box. The spinning cipher wheels would randomly select a different letter to represent the original letter. This substitute letter would then be typed out on the second typewriter. By this means, each letter of a message typed on the first typewriter would be changed into a randomly selected letter message on the second machine.

The cipher machine seemed foolproof. Instead of crack-ing a single code that applied to the entire message, an enemy would have to crack a different code for each letter. There was no logical way of predicting what a letter typed on the first typewriter might end up as on the second type-writer. Frequency charts were useless in trying to decipher the message. The encoded message might show the letter "A" twelve times in a row, and each "A" might stand for a different letter. The cipher machines could crank out these baffling codes in a matter of seconds and were not as sub-ject to the possibility of human error as were most codes. To decode the message, the receiver would consult a thick book of machine keys and then plug in wire connections according to the machine key for the day. The only possi-ble way of breaking the code was to reproduce the mes-sage on one of the Japanese Purple Code units.

Incredibly, the U.S. Navy's OP-20-G intelligence unit broke the system within a short time. With the assistance of information gathered by spies, a massive program led by intelligence officer William Friedman was able to build a replica of the Japanese Purple Code machine. The code was broken so quickly that the United States military actually received some strong signals that the Pearl Harbor attack was coming—but failed to act upon them.

So confident were the Japanese that their Purple Code was unbreakable that they did not alter their system even when the evidence should have made them suspicious. From very early in the war the United States was reading secret Japanese military orders right along with Japanese field commanders.

Cipher machines, however, were not readily available to every small unit of the Japanese military. Other, less elaborate codes had to be used in the field. The United States and its allies in the Pacific benefited from a stroke of luck in trying to lift the veil of secrecy from these messages.

In the early stages of the war, a New Zealand warship happened across—and sank—a lone Japanese submarine near the Solomon Islands. It was the sort of isolated engagement that happens often enough in wartime. Tiny skirmishes like this ordinarily had no military impact and were merely lumped together with hundreds of others in the battle reports. This particular submarine, however, was carrying more than 20,000 manuals describing Japan's latest, most complex field codes. The books themselves could have been replaced quickly and easily, but the Japanese knew only that this submarine did not arrive at its destination. They did not know whether the codebooks had fallen into Allied hands. Rather than run the risk of using a code that the enemy could easily solve, the Japanese had to revert to an older, less effective one.

A prime example of how the United States benefited from code-breaking efforts occurred when the Japanese were sweeping through the Pacific in the early stages of the war. The Japanese offensive ranged in a huge arc for thousands of miles, from Australia over to Hawaii and all the way up to the Alaskan coast. The thinly stretched U.S. forces had too few soldiers and too little equipment to protect all the islands that lay in the path of the offensive. The attacking Japanese, meanwhile, could concentrate their forces on one objective at a time.

The U.S. position was like having a small handful of guards to protect a hundred banks spread out over an entire state from a band of robbers. The guards could offer effective protection against attack only if they happened to be stationed at the bank that the robbers attacked. The odds against their choosing the right bank to defend were woefully slim, unless they could tap in to the robbers' conversations.

The success of American intelligence units in breaking Japanese codes allowed the U.S. military to do just that kind of eavesdropping. In fact, they were reading Japanese secret communications so easily that some of them wondered if the Japanese were laying a trap by purposely sending false information. On some occasions the Americans and Japanese read each other so well that they might as well have been exchanging notes. For example, shortly after U.S. intelligence learned of Japanese plans to attack Port Moresby, Japanese intelligence discovered that the Allies were gathering to defend the port.

But American code-breaking efforts got the upper hand

For much of the early part of the war, both sides were
"reading each other's mail" almost as quickly as it was sent.
(COURTESY OF THE LIBRARY OF CONGRESS)

in one of the most decisive sea battles of the war. As the
summer of 1942 approached, the U.S. military intercepted
messages whose content warned them that the Japanese
fleet was planning for major action. While this part of the
plan was easy to read, trying to predict where that attack
might come from was a different story. In addition to their
normal codes, the Japanese used separate code names for
locations. The Americans knew that the target of the next
Japanese attack was a place code-named "AF." But despite
all their efforts, they could not figure out what "AF" meant.
Time was beginning to run out on the code-breakers. The
Japanese could strike at any moment.

Commander Rochefort, an intelligence officer stationed at Pearl Harbor, devised a clever plan to solve the

mystery of AF. His scheme was to turn Japan's own code-cracking skills to his own advantage. The commander of each defensive outpost that lay in the path of a potential Japanese advance was told to send a prearranged false message. Each was to report on some particular matter supposedly causing problems. Then the intelligence units listened in on Japanese communications-relay posts to see what would happen.

A few days later, American radio monitors picked up a report that relayed a message, picked up from U.S. forces on AF, which said that the facility was facing a shortage of drinking water. This drinking-water story was the false report sent by the commander of U.S. forces at Midway Island. Obviously, then, AF meant Midway Island, a small but strategic island northwest of Hawaii. The United States quickly called up some of its naval fleet from the South Pacific to help meet the coming attack.

The Japanese ships steaming toward Midway Island shut off their radios. Although this handicapped their own vital communications, they believed it was worth it to keep their intentions a secret. All it did, however, was keep the Japanese in the dark, since the Americans knew what was coming. The U.S. Navy, forewarned of assault, inflicted heavy casualties on the Japanese forces. The Japanese lost more than 300 airplanes in the fighting around Midway Island on June 5–6, 1942, compared with fewer than 150 American losses. More important, 4 of the Japanese navy's 9 aircraft carriers were sunk in the fighting. This loss erased Japan's military advantage on the sea. Japanese industry was unable to rebuild the navy in time to combat the growing power of the United States. Never again did the Japanese have the firepower to range at will across the vast Pacific theater.

Early the next year, an intercepted message devastated the Japanese in a very different way. American intelligence decoded a top-secret communication from Japan's naval commander-in-chief, Admiral Isoroku Yamamoto. Encouraged by reports of success, Yamamoto planned a one-day stop at the Solomon Islands to boost the spirits of troops locked in bloody combat with U.S. Marines.

Yamamoto was a capable military leader, one whom the Japanese could not afford to lose. It was he who had devised the flawless attack on Pearl Harbor. Although Yamamoto was taking something of a risk by visiting the troops, it seemed a tiny one. He would never go near the actual fighting. The United States had no aircraft bases or carriers in the immediate area. It was possible for American fighter planes to reach him from a faraway base, but they would have too little fuel to patrol the skies for any length of time. The only way that they could possibly threaten Yamamoto was if they knew precisely what route he was traveling and when he was arriving. Even so, he would be protected by a strong escort of fighter planes.

Thanks to its intelligence operations, though, the United States *did* know exactly when Yamamoto was arriving and what route he would be taking. They also knew in what sort of craft he would be flying, and the number and types of planes in his escort. As a military combatant, Yamamoto was considered a fair target, and the United States went after him. The American planes would have to fly to the limit of their fuel tanks to reach his landing site and have enough left over to get home. They would have no time to circle, waiting for Yamamoto. If he was just a couple of minutes behind, the attempt would fail. But Yamamoto's reputation for sticking strictly to a schedule made the effort worthwhile.

On the morning of April 18, 1943, Yamamoto's escort brought him safely to his destination in the Solomon Islands. As Yamamoto's plane descended toward the runway, the escort broke away, their mission apparently accomplished without incident. Suddenly eighteen American P-38 Lightning aircraft streaked across the sky. Ignoring the belated efforts of the surprised escort to drive them off, they shot down the admiral's plane. Yamamoto was killed. Military experts agree that the Japanese missed his military expertise in the battles that followed.

Perhaps the most telling effect of American code-breaking was in the relatively unheralded submarine warfare. As a small island nation with few natural resources of its own, Japan had to depend on raw materials shipped from its new territories to supply its wartime industry. U.S. intelligence was able to piece together enough information from intercepted messages to determine routes and schedules of these merchant-marine vessels. Armed with this knowledge, American submarines prowled the shipping routes, picking off ships and then slinking deep under the water.

Most of Japan's merchant-marine fleet was destroyed. Nearly 1,200 Japanese cargo-carrying ships, weighing a total of 5 million tons, ended up on the bottom of the ocean. Along with these ships went the hopes of the Japanese military. By cutting off Japan's raw materials, the United States drastically slashed Japan's ability to produce military goods and equipment. While the United States was able to crank out new and better ships, planes, and military hardware for their troops, the Japanese were unable to replace destroyed and captured equipment.

When the United States finally took the offensive in 1944, intercepted messages frequently gave commanders access to enemy defensive formations and plans. American radio operators then listened to reports from Japanese commanders during and after the battles. These reports gave them an accurate picture of how the battles were going and what condition the enemy was in.

Military experts estimate that U.S. code-cracking efforts

Corporal Sam Begay translates a message coming in on his receiver. (COURTESY OF NATIONAL ARCHIVES)

shortened the war in the Pacific by at least a year. Some even speculate that the war might have turned out differently were it not for U.S. intelligence contributions.

The disasters that plagued the Japanese because of intercepted messages could just as easily have happened to the Americans had they relied on their standard methods of coding. The Navajo code, however, proved too difficult for the Japanese to break. Cloaked in a modified form of an ancient language, American military secrets remained safe.

▶ 7 ◀

Island-Hopping

AS HEARTENED AS THE code talkers were by their success in the Solomon Islands, they realized it was only a small first step on a long, perilous expedition across the Pacific.

The task of reclaiming the Pacific from the Japanese posed challenges that the U.S. military had never faced before. The Japanese offensive finished, Japan now dug in to protect its new empire from attack. The normal method of taking territory from an enemy was to stage a major ground campaign. An army would work at outflanking the enemy and gaining favorable terrain. That could not work against the far-flung island strongholds of the Japanese: It would be like attacking hundreds of separate, well-fortified castles, each protected by a vast moat called the Pacific Ocean.

Then there was the problem of air support. Head-on assaults against entrenched positions were bloody affairs. Unless supported by air strikes, they would cost the attackers a horrendous number of lives. Yet the islands held by the Japanese were often too far away for Allied planes to reach from their bases. Aircraft carriers could move some of the planes in closer, but not close enough to satisfy Allied commanders.

The Americans had to improvise a method of attacking these Japanese defenses. The solution was to send the marines on an "island-hopping" campaign through the Central Pacific. Ground troops, supported by air and sea power, would be ferried to the first objective. When that island was captured, the Americans could use it as an air and supply base for attacking the next island up the line.

This type of operation required rapid, secure communications between commanders on the ships and frontline units on the beaches. The Navajo code talkers, if they proved reliable, would be especially valuable in this type of campaign. But the Navajo code was still basically an experiment. There were doubts that a campaign as important as this could afford to take a chance with them. Battle often brought about situations that could not be anticipated in training. Radio operators occasionally had to improvise new terms to fit new situations. Those receiving the messages had to be able to react to these innovations in a fraction of a second. The slightest mistake in translation could send soldiers to their deaths.

Prior to the island-hopping campaign, marine divisions were asked to evaluate the Navajo code talkers' performance during the fighting in the Solomon Islands. The response was so glowing that it persuaded senior marine officers to recommend the use of code talkers for the island-hopping campaign. Two Navajos were assigned to each infantry and artillery battalion. To make sure that all operators were kept aware of the latest adjustments in the code, code talkers from various units were brought together every so often to check signals.

In November 1943, well over a year after the United States first landed troops at Guadalcanal, the American forces—with their Navajo communicators—moved into action. The first target was the Gilbert Islands, a widely spaced string of more than a dozen small islands that barely poked above the surface of the ocean northeast of the Solomons.

If all went well, the Gilberts would be an ideal testing ground for America's new amphibious tactics. Isolated outposts at the most exposed corner of Japan's empire, the Gilberts lay far from Japanese supply lanes, yet within easy reach of American bases. The islands were tiny, but militarily important because they could easily be converted to airstrips. The main objective of the U.S. attack was the Tarawa atoll, a ring of tiny islands, the most important of which was Betio. Betio was no more than five hundred yards wide and two miles long.

Betio was going to be either a cakewalk or a suicide mission, depending on whom you listened to. The Japanese commander believed that his 4,500 troops were so well dug in that "a million men cannot take Tarawa in a hundred years."[13] The defenses were indeed impressive, as photographs shot from overflying planes proved. The island was plastered with concrete blockhouses and pillboxes (small machine-gun shelters), some more than six-teen feet high.

On the other hand, the islands were nothing more than tiny wedges of coral covered with sand and coconut trees. They were so flat that they offered the defenders little protection against bombs and artillery shells. American planes and naval batteries opened the campaign by pound-ing Betio from one end to the other. More than 3,000 tons of explosives rained down on the tiny island. A later search found bomb fragments on every square yard of Be-tio. The marine troops approaching from the sea in their landing craft saw nothing but flames rising out of a thick cloud of dust. It was difficult to imagine that the defenders were in any shape to fight back against the American land-ing forces.

U.S. amphibious assault tactics, however, were far from perfect. Several waves of landing craft ran aground on a coral reef and were stranded far from the beach. The ma-rines were forced to wade for as much as half a mile through shallow water before reaching the beach, all the while offering a slow-moving target to the enemy. The Jap-anese were far from devastated by the pre-attack bombard-ment. Dug in behind coconut-log barriers, they aimed a murderous stream of fire at the marines wading toward the beach.

The landing craft in which Navajo code talker Jerry C. Begay, Sr., was riding made it past the reef, only to strike a pier instead of the beach. "The halftrack blew up," Begay recalled. "Instead of fighting, I helped those who were

The vast numbers of soldiers, supplies, and landing craft
used in amphibious assaults required tremendous coordination

floating around back to safety."[14] The spectacle of the dead and dying was terrible.

When the marines were finally able to claw their way inland the next morning, they ran into barbed-wire fences and more coconut logs. Those marines who tried to climb over the barriers faced withering fire from soldiers determined to die rather than surrender. "We had a hard time,"

and frequent communication to keep everything from falling into chaos. (COURTESY OF NATIONAL ARCHIVES)

according to Howard Billman, Jr. "Men were getting killed right and left."[15] Jerry Begay made it to the beach, was wounded in the third day of fighting, and was evacuated to a hospital ship.

Despite a large advantage in numbers and firepower, the marines suffered heavy losses before gaining control of the island. In four savage days of fighting over 1,000 of the

81

16,000 attackers were killed; over 2,000 others were wounded. Only 17 Japanese soldiers were taken prisoner. The rest of the defenders lay dead on the sand.

The marines learned a number of sobering lessons at Tarawa. A successful amphibious assault required meticulous planning and proper equipment. Good communications were also essential. Even on a battlefront as small as Betio, units had been scattered and cut off from their command groups. Communication between the men on the beaches and the attack coordinators had been spotty. The marines needed to learn how to make use of their code talkers, many of whom were still being assigned regular marine duty instead of doing what they'd been trained for.

After securing the Gilbert Islands, the marines moved to

U.S. Marines advance through the bomb-shredded palm trees of Tarawa. (COURTESY OF NATIONAL ARCHIVES)

the north. They were determined that the next target, the Marshall Islands, would not be so dearly bought. The Marshalls posed a similar challenge to the Gilberts. They were a series of several dozen flat, sandy islands whose highest point was only twenty-one feet above the ocean. They were less heavily fortified than Tarawa, however, and U.S. planning and tactics were better, as was communication on the front lines. In January and February 1944, the marines attacked and overran Japanese defenses on the islands.

Having stripped the Japanese of their outer ring of defenses, the marines now focused on piercing the next layer of the Japanese empire. The Mariana Islands lay roughly halfway between the Gilberts and Japan. The marines could expect far stiffer resistance and far greater numbers of Japanese troops concentrated here. The mountainous terrain would also pose a different challenge.

On June 15, 1944, the marines landed on the second-largest of the Marianas, Saipan, strategically important for its fine harbor. At about the same time, the Japanese navy suffered a crippling defeat in the Battle of the Philippine Sea; this loss cut off the defenders of the Marianas from reinforcements. Nestled into their network of caves on the rugged slopes, the 31,000 Japanese troops were determined to hold onto the island with their last breath.

At Saipan, the code talkers manned their stations under relentless fire. Besides carrying maps and escorting prisoners, troops, and civilians around the island, code talker Albert Smith provided a key communications link. "I oper-

Private First Class Cecil Trosip is dug into the sands of Saipan for protection from snipers as he cranks up his transmitter.
(COURTESY OF NATIONAL ARCHIVES)

ated the radio for the riflemen and was under fire myself while delivering messages."[16]

After three weeks of tough fighting, the remaining Japanese soldiers fixed their bayonets for a final charge. Their suicidal attack was repulsed, and on July 9, the marines hoisted the American flag to signal victory.

A couple of weeks later, another force of marines attacked the island of Tinian, just to the south of Saipan. Here the marines surprised the defenders with their "backdoor" landing. While the Japanese waited for the assault on the main beach, American troops streamed through a small beach directly behind them. As a result, Tinian was captured with little difficulty.

A third attack targeted the island of Guam, south of Saipan. The code talkers' work on this battlefront earned them some of their highest praise. According to Colonel Marlowe Williams, the code talkers "were invaluable throughout the assault on Guam."[17]

In each of these battles, from Tarawa to Guam, the Japanese were confounded by strange noises coming from American radios, such an unearthly collection of sounds that they were not even sure that what they heard was human speech. Whatever it was, they had no clue to how to begin to decipher it.

Unknown to the Japanese, the Navajos were coordinating the marines' attack. They relayed messages from the front lines so that commanding officers monitoring the battle would know who was low on ammunition and who needed medical assistance. They relayed information about enemy movements and artillery placements. Most important, they could provide this information without revealing anything to the enemy.

The Navajos' role in directing friendly artillery fire was especially critical. Early in the war, U.S. artillery shells frequently landed short of the target, so the marines had become reluctant to call in artillery fire on close enemy positions. Navajo code talkers could redirect such inaccuracies quickly. The Navajos themselves believed their most important role was in alerting the attack commanders of units or sections of the line that were in danger so that reinforcements could be brought in.

Typical of the service provided by the code talkers was their report of a Japanese attack force on Guam. A marine scouting force had discovered the Japanese about to descend upon an exposed American unit. Code talker George H. Kirk, Sr., recalled that the code talkers quickly relayed the information to a battleship and two artillery units, along with the exact location of the Japanese. The resulting bombardment was so accurate that the "the Japanese were wiped out and our commander, Major General Erskine, was saved by our language."[18]

The Navajos were equally valuable in communicating top-secret information from central command to the front lines. The words "New Mexico" or "Arizona" coming over the radio of a frontline unit meant that a message was about to be broadcast in Navajo code. The speed with which the Navajos could communicate allowed commanders quickly to recall troops that were drifting into areas targeted for artillery blasts.

As the efficiency and effectiveness of the Navajos were demonstrated time after time in these early campaigns, more code talkers were brought into use. The code-talker system became the marines' primary means of communication, especially for units fighting in small, isolated areas where there was no time to mess around with time-consuming codes and deciphering. Commanders came to trust the code talkers so thoroughly, especially for crucial messages that needed to be sent during actual combat, that they would use no one but a code talker to transmit by radio. In many cases, the messages never would have been received in time had the marines relied on the more time-consuming ciphering and deciphering of traditional codes.

Because the Navajos had to send and deliver these messages from the front lines, they ran a high risk of being shot. Code talker William Dean Wilson fell into a foxhole with live Japanese soldiers on Tarawa and survived to tell the tale. Bill Henry Toledo's radio was knocked out during the fighting on Guam. Forced to run a message from the front line to the beach command post, Toledo narrowly escaped a volley of shots from a sniper who had been waiting for him. Jack Morgan was nearly shot while on guard duty one night on Guam. Seven code talkers were killed in action.

The sacrifices made by the marines in the island-hopping campaign did more than simply clear a few islands of Japanese invaders. American bulldozers leveled enough land on the Marianas to build a huge complex of airfields. It was from these runways that America's brand-new long-range bombers, the huge B-29s, took off on their 3,000-mile round trips to blast military targets in Tokyo and other Japanese cities. Late in the war, the *Enola Gay* would lift off a runway on Tinian and fly toward the city of Hiroshima. In its bomb bay was the first atomic bomb ever used in warfare, the weapon that brought the long war to a quick and horrifying end.

The war was not over for the marines with victory in the Marianas and the subsequent triumph of the army in the Philippines. The worst was yet to come. No marine would ever forget the fight for Iwo Jima. As a bright object shines even more brightly against the darkest of backgrounds, the Navajo code talkers would shine brightest in this most savage of all World War II battles.

► 8 ◄

The Battle of Sulfur Island:
The Code Talkers' Finest Hour

"IWO JIMA" MEANS "SULFUR Island," and the marines considered it a fittingly distasteful name for the place. Like many Pacific battlegrounds, Iwo Jima barely shows up on a large map. It stretches about five miles from north to south and measures only two and a half miles at its widest point. Unlike the flat sands of Tarawa or the mountainous jungles of Saipan, Iwo Jima juts out of the water like a craggy stone.

The marines' next target was far from an island paradise. Vegetation was sparse. The air reeked from the sulfur springs. There was not so much as a single river, stream, or even drinkable spring on the island.

Iwo Jima offered only two possible approaches for an attacking force; neither was inviting. The western shore provided easier terrain for ground forces, but the pounding surf could wreak havoc on landing boats. The eastern side offered calmer waters, but an ominous beachhead for the ground troops. The beach sloped sharply upward in a series of exposed terraces that even tracked vehicles such as tanks would have trouble climbing.

Iwo Jima was defended by 22,000 Japanese soldiers commanded by one of Japan's most capable leaders, General Tadamichi Kuribayashi. The general had been told that Iwo Jima held the key to Japan's future. He did not have to be told that it was to be defended to the death. Kuribayashi vowed that if the Americans wanted Iwo Jima, they would pay a terrible price. Working like frenzied moles, his troops dug in to prepare a killing field such as the world had never seen before. Caves connected by miles of tunnels were dug and blasted into the porous volcanic rock. Machine-gun nests, mortar pits, pillboxes, and block-houses were anchored into the rock. Mine fields were laid.

The tiny island cast a long and dark shadow over the marine commanders who sized it up from afar. But the place could not be avoided. Iwo Jima sat right in the middle of the bombing route between the Mariana Islands and Tokyo. Japanese spotters on Iwo Jima could warn the mainland well in advance whenever the B-29s roared overhead. Japanese fighters could take off from Iwo Jima's three runways to intercept the bombers. Several Japanese bombing raids from Iwo Jima struck Allied airfields in the Marianas, destroying or damaging dozens of the giant bombers.

On the B-29s' first bombing run from the Marianas to Japan, on November 17, 1944, one of the superfortresses plummeted into the sea on its return flight. A week later, two more B-29s were lost after completing their bombing missions. If the United States controlled Iwo Jima, crippled bombers could use it as an emergency landing spot. Iwo Jima could also provide a base for smaller, short-range fighters that could provide an escort for the bombers.

American planes bombed Iwo Jima for seventy-four consecutive days in an attempt to soften the island's defenses. Yet at the end of that time, aerial photographs showed that Kuribayashi's defenses were stronger than they had been before the bombing started.

In February 1945, the largest force of marines ever committed to action sailed for Iwo Jima. One of the code talkers, looking out over an ocean cluttered with American warships bristling with guns, could not imagine how the United States could lose. Several commanders agreed. They expected to be in control of Iwo Jima within a week, ten days at the most. Others were queasy about what lay ahead.

While most of the troops could do little but await the designated attack day, several code talkers had to perform yet another demonstration of their skill. Despite the high marks that the code talkers had received all through the island campaigns, there were still doubters. In Major General Keller Rockey's command ship, the U.S.S. *Cecil*, a team of four Navajos was pitted against four marine signal officers. Again, the Navajos easily won the encounter and with it, the responsibility for communicating orders and information on Iwo Jima.

On February 19, the navy let loose with the most furious barrage of the war. In half an hour they lobbed more than eight thousand volleys onto the beaches and hills of Iwo

Jima. At eight-thirty in the morning, the first wave of 1,400 marines was ready to go in.

The plan called for the first assault to clear out a beachhead against expected heavy resistance. Once that was accomplished, the code talkers could come in with the next waves of soldiers. The marines would then fortify their lines for the Japanese counterattack that would be launched to drive them from the beaches. That basic script had been followed in every landing since Tarawa.

The first marines met virtually no resistance. One unit raced across the island to the western shore in an hour and a half, blowing up many Japanese pillboxes along the way. As the main body of marines advanced several hundred yards up the sandy terraces, some even dared to hope

The landing beach at Iwo Jima, littered with equipment. Mount Suribachi rises up in the background. (COURTESY OF NATIONAL ARCHIVES)

that the Japanese had been nearly wiped out by the bombardment. But as the code talkers reached the supposedly "secure" beachhead, something obviously was wrong. General Kuribayashi had learned from those defeats on the beaches of Saipan and Guam. Now he crossed up the Americans by breaking with the Japanese tradition of defending the beaches. Instead he held back his troops and allowed the Americans to land. Once the beaches were crowded with soldiers, the unseen Japanese opened fire.

There was nowhere for the Americans to run and few places to hide. Trying to dig into the black volcanic sand was like digging into a pile of grain. The enemy fire was so heavy and so accurate that one marine was hit in both legs, then his shoulder, then a thigh. A fifth shell blew his watch away from his wrist. Somehow, he survived.

Those who did not survive included many marines who dove into pits and trenches along the beach. These supposedly safe havens turned out to be traps. The Japanese had fine-tuned their mortar sights to lob shells directly into those holes.

Thomas Begay was sent in to replace fellow code talker Paul Kinlacheeny, who was among those killed on the beach. "The first hour, I was with my radio, communicating with other floats," said Begay. "I was scared, very scared, mortars and artillery were landing everywhere, but I wasn't hit."[19] Begay, a very traditional Navajo, credited his survival to the ceremonies performed on his behalf by his family back home.

Newly arriving waves of marines, among them code talker Merril Sandoval, were also caught in the barrage.

"Our landing craft was hit sideways and overturned and we lost our equipment," remembered Sandoval.[20]

Bodies lay everywhere on the beach, along with the wreckage of burned and useless equipment. In many cases, nothing could be done for the wounded except to pull them into a foxhole and hope that a medic could arrive before it was too late. One American tank operator had to drive right over a pile of dead Americans in order to get his vehicle into the action. The marines, who at first had cheered the arrival of the tanks, began to curse them. The tanks attracted even more murderous fire, and many of the marines stayed as far away from them as they could.

An American reporter, observing from an airplane, reported that Iwo Jima looked like a fat, sizzling pork chop. Another witness wrote that he saw "more hell in there than I've seen in the rest of the war put together."[21]

In this grisly, terrifying uproar, the Navajo code talkers set up their radios and went to work. All communication from the command post at sea to the three divisional command posts on the beach was handled by Navajos. They directed gunfire from the ships and the airplanes toward hidden mortar and artillery pockets that they had detected. They relayed messages from air observers about enemy hazards and informed fellow marines of where artillery fire from the ships was being aimed.

The task was never more difficult than on the Iwo Jima beach. Somehow, while dodging mortar fire and ducking bullets, with the screams of the dying all around them, the Navajos had to recall instantly every word of the code and be able to improvise without delay when the need arose.

Marines crammed into a large foxhole on the beach at
Iwo Jima.

(COURTESY OF NATIONAL ARCHIVES)

They handled the task with incredible efficiency and courage. An officer in the Fifth Marine Division stated that during the chaotic first forty-eight hours of the Iwo Jima invasion, his command posts had six Navajo radio units working around the clock. "During that period, they sent and received more than 800 messages without error."[22]

One of the messages from the command center reached code talker Raphael Yazzie during a heavy exchange of gunfire on the front lines: "We received orders by radio to assist in the rescue of our platoon, which was under fire. We did, and got all of our men safely back to our regiment."[23] In the heat of battle, code talkers were called upon for other duties besides sending messages.

Nighttime offered no relief in the campaign to take Iwo Jima. The American forces continually braced themselves for the counterattack that usually followed a beach assault. Although the mass assault against the beach never came, individual Japanese attacks could and did come at any time. A "dead" soldier might suddenly jump up and start firing. Another might burst out of a cave. Edgy marines were poised to shoot at anything that moved. A marine who popped out of his foxhole in the darkness after accidentally dropping a live grenade was killed by his comrades' fire.

One code talker was crowded together with six others in a foxhole when they heard a rustling coming toward them. The marines came up firing only to discover that their enemy was a wild pig.

After fighting their way off the beach, the marines set their sights on Mount Suribachi, an extinct volcano on the southern tip of the island. Suribachi rose straight up from the sea to a height of 550 feet and was ringed with caves and tunnels. The marines advanced slowly in some of the grimmest fighting of the war, prying and blasting the defenders out of their holes one by one. But by the end of the first week, a group of marines reached the top and planted the U.S. flag in the mountain's soft volcanic rock. Word of Mount Suribachi's capture reached command headquarters via Navajo code.

The marines did not capture Iwo Jima in a week or ten days. Not until March 16, nearly a month after the initial assault, was the island declared secure, and scattered fighting continued for another two weeks after that. More than 6,800 U.S. soldiers died trying to take Sulfur Island. Nearly 20,000 others were wounded. Nearly all of the Japanese defenders perished.

There were two redeeming features of this terrible slaughter. One was the incredible bravery of those on both sides who were thrown into this caldron of death. Few human acts can measure up against the sacrifice of five marines who lost their lives smothering grenades so that their companions might live. The marine radio operators contributed their share of heroism at Iwo Jima. One radioman had his foot blown apart on the beach. Rather than calling for help, the man set up his radio right where he fell. There he sent and received messages until he passed out from pain and shock.

The other result of the battle for Iwo Jima was that it may actually have saved American lives. Scarcely a day went by when a sputtering, shredded B-29 bomber did not

Marines plant the U.S. flag after reaching the top of Mount Suribachi.

limp onto the runway at Iwo Jima. By the end of the war, the giant bombers had made 2,251 landings on Iwo Jima. Not all of these were so desperately disabled that they could not have made it back to the Mariana Islands bases. Not all of the 27,000 crewmen aboard these planes would have been killed if Iwo Jima had not been available. But U.S. Admiral Ernest King calculated that more military personnel were saved by Iwo Jima than were killed in taking it.

(COURTESY OF NATIONAL ARCHIVES)

These crewmen owed an unpayable debt to the marines. Many of them did not know until many years later, if ever, that part of that debt was owed to the Navajo code talkers. No one can measure exactly the contribution made by these Native Americans. But one guess came from one who was at the battle: Major Howard Conner, signal officer of the Fifth Marine Division. "Were it not for the Navajo code talkers, the Marines never would have taken Iwo Jima."[24]

► 9 ◄

Back Home

THE FINAL ISLAND BATTLEGROUND of the war was Okinawa, a large island 60 miles long and 18 miles wide in spots. Japan was by this time hopelessly outgunned by American military might, which grew daily. But the Japanese fought more ferociously than ever to hold on to Okinawa, less than 400 miles from the Japanese home islands. The Okinawa campaign raged for more than two months, during which American losses ran even higher than at Iwo Jima.

Once again, though, Navajo code talkers worked to keep losses to a minimum as they handled the bulk of the communications for the attacking force. Roy Hawthorne's patrol was trapped under a flurry of enemy fire for two days on Okinawa. "The antenna of my radio was shot off, but I was able to get a message through for reinforcements."[25]

Okinawa fell to American forces after a bloody struggle that left the marines wary of the next leg of the journey: an invasion of the main Japanese islands. As they waited on Okinawa in August 1945 for word of what was to happen next, a Navajo working the radio received a message. Instantly he leaped to his feet and started dancing. Pounding out a rhythm as he danced, he made his way to the officers' tents. There he broke the news that, following the atomic-bomb blasts destroying Hiroshima and Nagasaki, Japan had surrendered.

The Navajos came home bearing the scars of a terrible experience. Most tried to put the war of the *belegaana* behind them. Cleansing ceremonies such as the Enemy Way were performed to put them at ease. "Let the white way of life, and death, be now cast out of you," sang the Navajo singers.

Some felt cleansed enough to move on with their lives. Some did not.

Some Navajos would speak openly of their experiences, even finding humorous edges to the most terrifying of situations. There were those who had seen the benefits that education had brought to the *belegaana*, and they wished to bring those to the Navajo.

Others would say nothing of the war, could not bear to read about it or watch any kind of war movie. Some carried wounds, both of the body and the spirit, with them for the rest of their lives.

However the war had affected the Navajo code talkers, it appeared to have had no impact on the way they were treated by American society once they were back home on the reservation. The Navajos who had fought as equals among the *belegaana* found themselves back at the bottom of society. These heroes of the U.S. war effort could not

Group photo of a marine unit of Navajo code talkers.

(COURTESY OF NATIONAL ARCHIVES)

vote in some states. They could not compete with the *belegaana* for good jobs. Their land was poor, their people hungry and illiterate. Little money was available for education.

The code talkers were treated with great respect by their own people. When some of the war veterans spoke of the need for the Navajos to educate their young and to take a more active role in governing their affairs and controlling their own resources, people listened. One of the Navajo nation's first chairmen, Peter MacDonald, was a marine code talker.

But among their *belegaana* neighbors, the sacrifices of the code talkers went largely unrecognized, thanks to the veil of secrecy that had continued to cover the entire operation. The Navajos were asked to avoid publicity after the war in case the Navajo code was needed again in the future. (In fact, some Navajo code talkers were used in Korea in the 1950s and in Vietnam in the 1960s.)

Modest about their role in the Pacific war, the Navajo did as they were asked. Many of the *belegaana* marines who had fought with the Navajo and witnessed their courage remained ignorant of what the Navajo radio operators had been doing in the field. Even today, one can read stacks of thick books about the Pacific war, about Iwo Jima and Tarawa, even about World War II military communication, without seeing any mention of the Navajo code talkers.

Not until the code talkers were specially recognized by a reunion of the Fourth Marine Division Association in 1969 did the Navajo war effort receive national recognition. More than twenty-five years after the fighting stopped, the United States belatedly took notice of the service offered by the Navajos. In 1971, President Richard Nixon awarded the Navajo code talkers a special certificate thanking them for their "patriotism, resourcefulness, and courage." Ironically, "patriotism" is one of the few English words for which the Navajo language does not have an equivalent. Five years later the code talkers, financed with funds raised by a Phoenix television station, participated in the July Fourth Bicentennial parade in Washington, D.C.

In May 1982, the U.S. Senate passed a motion declaring August 14, 1982, National Code Talkers Day. Arizona Senator Dennis DeConcini had this to say in sponsoring the bill: "Since the Code Talkers' work required absolute secrecy, they never enjoyed the national acclaim they so much deserved. I do not want this illustrious yet unassuming group of Navajo Marines to fade into history without notice."[26]

DeConcini's words were spoken nearly 120 years after the Long Walk, when the U.S. government nearly caused the entire Navajo people to fade into history without notice. One hundred twenty years later, the United States acknowledged how fortunate it is that the Navajo nation, now 150,000 strong, has survived.

Notes

1. Jules Loh, *Lords of the Earth* (New York: Crowell, 1971), p. 60.
2. Doris Paul, *Navajo Code Talkers* (Philadelphia: Lippincott, 1973), p. 2.
3. Ibid., p. 4.
4. Alison Bernstein, *American Indians and World War II* (Norman, Okla.: University of Oklahoma Press, 1991), p. 48.
5. Paul, op. cit., p. 19.
6. Ibid., p. 20.
7. William E. Hafford, "The Navajo Code Talkers," *Arizona Highways*, February 1989.
8. Kenji Kawano, *Warriors: Navajo Code Talkers* (Tucson, Ariz.: Northland, 1990), p. 26.
9. Paul, op. cit., p. 32.
10. Marley Shebala, "One Man Remembers His Radio," *Farmington Daily Times*, December 2, 1990.
11. Hafford, op. cit.

12. Ibid.

13. Martin Russ, *Line of Departure: Tarawa* (New York: Doubleday, 1975), p. 177.

14. Kawano, op. cit., p. 25.

15. Ibid., p. 34.

16. Ibid., p. 83.

17. Paul, op. cit., p. 98.

18. Kawano, op. cit., p. 61.

19. Ibid., p. 28.

20. Ibid., p. 80.

21. Richard F. Newcomb, *Iwo Jima* (New York: Doubleday, 1965), p. 117.

22. Paul, op. cit., p. 73.

23. Kawano, op. cit., p. 99.

24. Shirley Belleranti, "The Code That Couldn't Be Cracked," *The Retired Officer,* November 1984.

25. Kawano, op. cit., p. 48.

26. Belleranti, op. cit.

Bibliography

Navajo Code Talkers

Belleranti, Shirley. "The Code That Couldn't Be Cracked."
The Retired Officer. November 1984.

Bernstein, Alison. *American Indians and World War II.*
Norman, Okla.: University of Oklahoma Press, 1991.

Hafford, William E. "The Navajo Code Talkers." *Arizona
Highways.* February 1989.

Kawano, Kenji. *Warriors: Navajo Code Talkers.* Tucson,
Ariz.: Northland, 1990.

Paul, Doris. *Navajo Code Talkers.* Philadelphia: Lippincott,
1973.

Navajo Culture

America's Fascinating Indian Heritage. Pleasantville, N.Y.:
Reader's Digest, 1978.

Iverson, Peter. *The Navajo Nation.* Westport, Conn.: Green-
wood Press, 1981.

Kluckhohn, Clyde, and Dorothea Leighton. *The Navajo.* New York: Natural History Library, 1970.

Loh, Jules. *Lords of the Earth.* New York: Crowell, 1973.

O'Dell, Scott. *Sing Down the Moon* (fiction). New York: Dell, 1970.

The World of American Indians. Washington, D.C.: National Geographic, 1974.

WORLD WAR II CRYPTOGRAPHY

Khan, David. *The Codebreakers: The Story of Secret Writing.* New York: Macmillan, 1976.

Norman, Bruce. *Secret Warfare: The Battle of Codes and Ciphers.* Washington, D.C.: Acropolis, 1973.

Van Der Rhoer, Edward. *Deadly Magic.* New York: Scribners, 1978.

WORLD WAR II BATTLES — PACIFIC

Coggins, Jack. *The Campaign for Guadalcanal.* New York: Doubleday, 1972.

Kent, Graeme. *Guadalcanal: Island Ordeal.* New York: Ballantine, 1971.

Newcomb, Richard F. *Iwo Jima.* New York: Doubleday, 1965.

Russ, Martin. *Line of Departure: Tarawa.* New York: Doubleday, 1975.

Tregaskis, Richard. *Guadalcanal Diary.* New York: Random House, 1943.

Index